Breaking the Cycle

Breaking the Cycle

Navigating Unintentional Damage and Cultivating Healing

Lianne Terry

authors
AND CO.

First published in Great Britain in 2024
by Authors & Co.
www.authorsandco.pub

ISBN 978-1-915771-68-1 (paperback)

Disclaimer

This book is intended to be a helpful guide on the topics discussed. It is not written as a diagnostic tool or a treatment for any condition. Please be sure to consult a medical practitioner before you make any decisions that may affect your health.

For my own little family; my supportive wife, Amanda, my fantastic daughters, Esmé and Elodie, and my own amazing mum.

Contents

Introduction: The Influence of Our Family

The Root of Our Challenges

Many of you are carrying anxieties, depression, insecurities or intense emotions, without an immediately evident source. There's no significant trauma to point to, no dreadful parental anecdotes or adverse life events to explain the origins of these unsettling emotions, so, the question is, where do these issues originate from?

I believe I have the answer, and it lies within your family. In Philip Larkin's poem, *This Be the Verse*, he talks about how our parents mess us up, and although often unintentional, I believe this to be true.

Our families wield a significant influence on us, and this influence is not always positive. Our families can inadvertently cause us the most harm despite their good intentions. What makes this difficult is our reluctance to acknowledge that our families have been a source of discomfort or pain. This doesn't mean that we must be angry with or hate our families, or that they are bad people – as parents and siblings, most of us do our best – but we often don't recognise, address or process this impact.

As a result of carrying this unprocessed pain with you, you can experience challenges that constantly affect your daily life. You might exhibit behaviours, emotions or cognitions without understanding their origins or how to modify or manage them – we may remain unaware of the source of our distress. Since our families shape us from an early age, their influence becomes deeply embedded, making it complex to unravel.

I'd venture to say that we have all been influenced by our families in ways that have left us grappling with issues. These issues don't necessarily stem from major traumatic events (though they leave undeniably significant marks) but rather from small, unnoticed aspects. These subtle nuances seep into our behaviours, becoming integral parts of us and yielding far-reaching consequences. These consequences manifest as anxiety, insecurity, depression, strained relationships, difficulties in decision-making, conflict resolution problems and the list goes on. Whilst they might not always seem substantial or vital enough to address directly, they seriously impact our ability to find contentment and lead joyful, satisfying lives.

Becoming Authentically Ourselves

To mitigate the impact of these familial wounds, our first step is recognition - understanding them intimately. I believe that knowledge equates to empowerment. By knowledge, I refer to self-awareness - understanding ourselves, our history, our experiences and the effects they've had on us. This knowledge will illuminate the path to processing, moving forward and liberating ourselves from pain and discomfort.

Throughout this book, we'll embark on a journey together, exploring the factors that might have shaped you, and initiating the healing process for those wounds. By engaging with your inner child, you'll address the root causes and finally lay your uneasy emotions to rest. Inner child work acknowledges that adult thoughts, feelings and behaviours often stem from childhood experiences. It empowers us to reconnect with our past selves, offering a chance for healing and self-guidance.

So, let's delve deep and acquaint ourselves with our inner children. Let's examine our relationships with our families and comprehend how they've contributed to shaping our identities. We can then decide if this identity still aligns with who we aspire to be, or if we wish to shed elements of ourselves that originated from external sources. This journey isn't about blaming our families or vilifying them; it's about tracing the origins of our behavioural patterns and making positive changes.

As a counsellor, I've had the privilege of assisting more than 250 clients over six years on a transformative journey. Together, we've delved into the origins of their pain and collaboratively transitioned towards healthier perspectives. My commitment to understanding family dynamics led me to further studies, aiding me in recognizing the roots of my own behaviours and catalysing positive change within myself. Through interactions with clients, friends and family, it's become evident to me that most of us have room for growth in this area, and I firmly believe that focusing on it can enhance your lives, as it has my own.

My personal experience involves a typical upbringing and a relatively content family life. However, certain aspects instilled by my parents and siblings have significantly shaped who I am. For instance, I wasn't taught how to sit with my uncomfortable or challenging emotions. My mother, to shield me from pain, would resort to distraction or comfort - a common parental instinct. Unfortunately, this approach didn't equip me with the skills to manage profound emotions. As an adult, I recognised my avoidance of discomfort and embarked on a journey to learn how to confront it. This isn't about casting blame, on my mother; it's about breaking cycles, challenging old ways and making positive change.

I've since walked this path alongside numerous clients, supporting them as they navigate the unfamiliar terrain of facing emotions like sadness, grief, anger, loneliness and fear for the first time. This example underscores how families can profoundly influence us and it's one small facet among many others.

Positive Transformation Awaits

As you engage with this book and delve into self-discovery, you'll embark on a journey of profound growth. Here's what lies ahead:

- **Enhanced Self-Awareness:** By delving into the depths of your being, you'll cultivate deeper self-awareness. This process can unveil hidden strengths and aspirations, offering insight into how your family has influenced you. This newfound self-understanding will shed light on the origins of issues like anxiety, depression, low self-esteem and emotional struggles. Armed with this knowledge, you'll be poised to address and alleviate these challenges.
- **Healing Your Inner Child and Shadow Self:** Through recognising and nurturing your inner child and shadow's needs and emotions, you'll cultivate self-compassion and self-care. This nurturing will foster an environment of kindness and empathy towards yourself, contributing to heightened self-esteem.
- **Conscious Behaviour Shifts:** Armed with self-awareness, you'll identify your behavioural patterns, enabling you to make intentional choices to either embrace or modify them. Awareness of how past experiences colour your present interactions will guide you toward healthier communication and relationship dynamics. Additionally, understanding your

attachment style will empower you to cultivate a more secure attachment through deliberate effort.

- **Emotional Liberation:** By allowing the release of long-suppressed emotions from childhood, you'll make space for emotional healing. This process will diminish emotional triggers by addressing their root causes. Strategies to manage challenging situations will emerge, fostering resilience and navigation skills. Clinging to intense emotions can result in stress, anxiety and even physical issues. By liberating these emotions, you'll unburden yourself, cultivating a positive outlook and heightened emotional well-being.
- **Embracing Acceptance:** Acknowledging the wounds and issues originating from your family is a vital step toward reflection and growth. Viewing these issues through an empathic lens enables acceptance and judgment-free acknowledgement. This perspective empowers you to effectively confront and overcome challenges.

This journey is about empowering yourself with self-awareness, compassion and the tools to overcome the hurdles woven into your past. By embracing this transformation, you pave the way for a more fulfilling and empowered life.

The individuals I collaborate with in therapy often arrive with an array of emotional struggles – anxiety, depression, self-esteem challenges and more. While some carry traumatic experiences, many are unable to pinpoint the roots of their difficulties. They exhibit patterns of negative relationships or behaviours but are unable to discern the origins of these patterns.

Employing the techniques detailed in this book, I guide them through a process of heightened self-awareness. Together, we embark on a journey to process and release family wounds that have been buried in their subconscious. Witnessing the profound shifts my clients undergo is inspiring. They make incredible strides, shedding detrimental patterns, pardoning wounds they weren't even conscious of and constructing lives brimming with contentment and purpose.

I've witnessed clients beat anxiety, triumph against depression, conquer addiction and eating disorders, bolster self-esteem and relinquish the grip of pain. In this process, they rediscover their authentic selves and build anew.

Moreover, I've embarked on my own voyage to comprehend my personal wounds, to unravel the origins of my anxieties and self-esteem struggles and to navigate them toward becoming my true self.

This shared journey of growth and healing forms the crux of my practice, guiding my clients toward transformation and authenticity.

The Power of Healing and Authentic Living

Drawing from a comprehensive survey I conducted, I discovered that a staggering 75% of us bear traces of childhood pain. Remarkably, this is true even when 95% of our families were well-intentioned and composed of good-hearted individuals. This revelation underscores a significant truth: while most of us hail from loving families, many of us carry latent wounds that yearn for healing.

By embarking on a journey of self-discovery and tracing back these wounds to their origins, we unearth a pathway to authenticity and happiness. This process illuminates the way forward - one that enables us to release burdens, reconcile with our past, break cycles and step into lives that resonate with our true selves. It's an opportunity to rise above the echoes of the past and craft a future marked by fulfilment and genuine joy.

The Wealth of Knowledge Awaiting You

Within the pages of this book, you will unlock a wealth of insights and tools to facilitate profound personal growth:

- **Understanding Family Influence:** You will explore how your family has uniquely influenced and shaped you. Armed with this knowledge, you'll make informed decisions about retaining, releasing, or altering these influences.
- **Attachment Styles and Relationships:** Gain an enriched comprehension of your attachment

style and how it shapes your relationships. Dive into your core beliefs and learn how to modify them if they no longer serve your best interests.

- **Inner Child Connection:** This journey will guide you to connect with your inner child, acknowledge their emotions and process past pains. By nurturing and reparenting your inner child, you'll pave the way for emotional healing.
- **Generational Impacts:** Explore the broad influence of generational shifts, from technology gaps to changing work ethics and educational goals. Assess how these factors have played into your life and determine whether you'd like to lessen their impact.
- **Boundaries and Personal Growth:** Learn about the importance of establishing and maintaining healthy boundaries for your personal development.
- **Love Languages:** Discover your love languages and decipher how you both give and receive love to foster stronger connections.
- **Individual Family Members:** Delve into the impacts of different family members on your life. Recognise their influences and engage in activities to heal and enact positive change.
- **Diverse Family Structures:** You'll explore the impacts of different relationships and dynamics, which will guide you toward healing and transformation.
- **Navigating Family Issues:** Encounter insights into diverse family issues and their potential

effects. Engage in reflections to process these challenges and pave the way forward towards a happier future.

In essence, this book offers a roadmap to understanding, healing and growth. By delving into each facet, you'll foster a profound connection with yourself and your history, ultimately steering yourself toward a life of authenticity, contentment and positive transformation.

Are you prepared to embark on a journey? It won't always be an easy one, you will discover new and interesting things about yourself and confront challenging truths. Nonetheless, it will be a rewarding trip and it will help you to put difficult emotions to rest.

To be frank, I firmly believe that our families have all affected us and caused us pain. Let's embark on a journey together to repair that damage, untangle our thought processes and emotions and weave them back together in a pattern that is logical and brings happiness. Let's break cycles and make a positive change.

Are you ready?

Part 1

Understanding Yourself

Chapter 1
Attachment Theory

Attachment is an emotional bond that forms between individuals. British psychologist, John Bowlby, is credited with pioneering attachment theory, which focuses on understanding the dynamics of this emotional bond or connection and how it impacts us throughout our lives.

Mary Ainsworth expanded on Bowlby's work and her "Strange Situation" study was a significant milestone in the field of attachment theory. Conducted in the 1970s, the study involved observing children aged between twelve and eighteen months in a controlled situation where they were briefly left alone and then reunited with their mothers. The results of this study led to the identification of three primary attachment styles: secure attachment, anxious attachment and avoidant attachment.

The fourth attachment style, known as disorganised attachment, was added by Main and Solomon in 1986. Other studies have corroborated these findings on attachment, solidifying our understanding of the four attachment styles that remain central in our discussions of attachment theory today.

Focussing on Bowlby, he proposed that attachment behaviours in small children are instinctive and rooted in evolution. According to his theory, these attachment behaviours have developed over time through natural selection because they enhance a child's chances of survival. In a nutshell, attachment behaviours, such as seeking proximity to a parent or caregiver, showing distress when separated and finding comfort in reunion, are not learned behaviours but are innate and instinctive. They serve as a fundamental foundation for forming relationships throughout our lives.

These instincts can manifest in various ways, leading to the four primary attachment styles. These styles influence how you approach relationships and navigate emotional connections with others and exert a lasting impact on your social and emotional development.

1. Secure Attachment: A Foundation for Healthy Relationships

Those of you with secure attachment are happy, social and connected; you understand and can express your emotions. Exhibiting a range of positive traits in your relationships as children and into adulthood, secure attachment serves as a strong foundation for forming and maintaining healthy, fulfilling relationships. It enables you, as individuals, to navigate emotional connections with ease, fostering mutual trust, understanding and emotional support.

To nurture secure attachment in children, certain conditions need to be met, including ensuring the child feels safe and protected, making sure they feel seen and understood, providing the child with comfort and reassurance when needed, as well as conveying the child's value and importance and supporting their curiosity and exploration.

In adulthood, those with a secure attachment style, often exhibit the following signs:

- The ability to regulate emotions effectively
- Goal-oriented behaviour, a clear sense of purpose
- The capacity to form trusting bonds
- Effective communication of their needs and emotions
- A belief in their ability to influence their environment
- A willingness to seek and provide emotional support
- Comfort with closeness and interdependence in relationships
- The ability to be content when alone
- The capacity for self-reflection and a positive self-view

2. Anxious/Preoccupied Attachment: The Quest for Consistency

Anxious attachment is one of the three insecure attachment styles and like the others, it takes shape in early childhood. This attachment style often arises due to inconsistent parenting. This means that the parents or caregivers are sometimes supportive and responsive to the child's needs, but at other times, they appear disconnected or unresponsive.

The key feature of this inconsistency is that the child finds it challenging to predict how their parents will respond to their needs in the future. This unpredictability creates a sense of insecurity and anxiety in the child, as they struggle to understand and anticipate their caregivers' reactions.

The development of an anxious attachment style can be influenced by other factors, including the needs of the parent or caregiver. When a parent seeks excessive closeness with a child to fulfil their own emotional needs, it can lead to the child developing an anxious attachment style. These parents appear over-protective, hovering or excessively anxious about their child's well-being.

This dynamic often reflects the parent's anxious attachment style, which they have inherited from their own family of origin. The continuity of these behavioural patterns across generations is a significant aspect of attachment theory. Parents who have an anxious attachment style themselves struggle with their insecurities and fears of rejection or abandonment, which can then be projected onto their children.

As a result, children raised by parents with anxious attachment tendencies internalise a sense of emotional unpredictability and insecurity, which can influence their attachment style and emotional experiences in their adult relationships. Understanding these patterns and their origins is a crucial step in the journey towards developing more secure and healthy attachments.

In summary, individuals who develop an anxious attachment style have experienced:

- Inconsistent responsiveness
- Disconnection or emotional distance
- Preoccupation or intrusiveness

Recognising Anxious Attachment Characteristics

Identifying an anxious attachment style often involves recognising certain key characteristics and behaviours in yourself. Common traits associated with an anxious attachment style are:

- **High Regard for Others, Low Self-Esteem** – They tend to think highly of others but have lower self-esteem themselves. They question their own worth and value in relationships.
- **Sensitivity to Others' Needs But Insecure About Your Own Worth** – They are highly sensitive and attuned to the needs of others

whilst feeling insecure about their own worth within relationships and friendships.

- **Self-Blame for Rejection or Unmet Needs** - When faced with rejection or unmet needs, they often blame themselves for the perceived shortcomings in relationships.
- **Constant Need for Reassurance** - They require frequent reassurance that they are loved, valued and considered good enough.
- **Jealousy and Suspicion** - They have a fear of abandonment, leading to jealousy or suspicion in relationships.
- **Preoccupation with Relationships** - They are preoccupied with their relationships and have difficulty being alone or independent.
- **Desire for Intimacy and Closeness** - They seek intimacy and closeness in their relationships to an excessive degree.
- **Emotional Dependency** - They rely on partners or others for emotional stability.
- **Emotional Rollercoaster** -Anxiety, stress and unhappiness characterise their emotional experience in relationships, leading to an emotional rollercoaster effect.
- **Intense Fear of Being Alone or Rejected** - Their fear of being alone or rejected can be intense, and they view the presence of their loved one as a cure for these fears.
- **Uncertainty About Love** - They feel unsure about whether they are loved or whether romantic partners are committed.

Recognising these characteristics can be a crucial first step in understanding and addressing an anxious attachment style. It can pave the way for personal growth, self-awareness and the development of more secure and fulfilling relationships.

3. Avoidant/Dismissive Attachment: Seeking Independence

Avoidant attachment is another of the insecure attachment types. It often develops due to parents or caregivers being emotionally distant or a family environment that doesn't encourage or tolerate the expression of emotions. Parents with avoidant tendencies have expectations of independence and emotional toughness from their children.

Key characteristics of the environment where an avoidant attachment will grow include:

- **Emotional Distance** - Parents or caregivers with avoidant tendencies are physically present but emotionally distant. They avoid emotional intimacy and will not be attuned to their child's emotional needs.
- **Independence Expectation** - These parents expect their children to be self-sufficient and tough and discourage emotional dependency.
- **Reserved Behaviour** - Caregivers with avoidant attachment are reserved and not openly expressive of emotions themselves.

- **Lack Of Support** - When the child reaches out for support or affection, caregivers back off or respond with emotional detachment.

Recognising Avoidant Attachment Characteristics

An avoidant attachment type can be recognised through the following characteristics:

- **Self-Confidence** - They exhibit self-confidence and a positive self-image.
- **Sociable and Independent** - They appear easy-going, sociable, and independent. They will often have a wide circle of friends or sexual partners.
- **High Self-Esteem** - They tend to have higher self-esteem and do not rely on others for reassurance or validation.
- **Emotional Control** - They appear in control of their emotions and find it challenging to express deep emotional vulnerability.
- **Barriers to Depth** - They put up emotional barriers when it comes to deep emotional intimacy.
- **Avoidance of Closeness** - They avoid strong displays of closeness and intimacy, often maintaining a certain emotional distance.
- **Reluctance to Emotional Intimacy** - They end relationships when they feel they are becoming too emotionally intimate or vulnerable.

- **Belief In Independence** - They believe they don't need emotional intimacy and prioritise independence in their relationships.

Again, recognising these traits in yourself can be the first step towards understanding and addressing avoidant attachment tendencies and seeking out more fulfilling relationships.

4. Disorganised/Fearful Attachment: A Complex Challenge

Disorganised or fearful attachment is one of the more complex and challenging attachment styles. It is often, but not always observed in individuals who have experienced physical, verbal or sexual abuse in childhood or have witnessed these traumatic experiences inflicted on others by their caregivers. This attachment style develops when caregivers who are supposed to be a source of safety and security become a source of fear and unpredictability.

Key characteristics of disorganised attachment include:

- **Craving Belonging but Fearing Intimacy** - They crave a sense of belonging and a desire to love and be loved, however, they are simultaneously afraid to let anyone get too close emotionally.
- **Fear of Being Hurt** - They fear that people close to them will hurt them emotionally or physically.

- **Anticipating Rejection** - They anticipate rejection and act in ways that contribute to self-fulfilling cycles of rejection.
- **Negative Self-View and Distrust** - They hold negative views of both themself and others, rooted in the belief that relationships are inherently unreliable or unsafe.
- **Higher Risk of Developing Mental Health Issues** - They have a higher risk of developing mental health issues due to the complex emotional challenges it presents.

My client, Maisie, was raised in a household where if she was well-behaved, she was shown love, but if she wasn't, the love was withdrawn, her emotional needs were no longer considered and if any emotion was displayed it was quickly shut down. This led to her feeling unsafe to express her emotions at all. As a result, Maisie became afraid of her primary caregiver, her mum. As her brother was a calm, quiet child, he wasn't as impacted, which led to Maisie feeling excluded from the family and resulted in her developing a disorganised attachment type.

In early adulthood, Maisie's disorganised attachment impacted her relationships. She felt extremely jealous and insecure and was often controlling or manipulative, however, she never allowed herself to be vulnerable and had many protective mechanisms in place.

Through personal development work, using lots of self-reflection and learning about the subconscious mind Maisie has healed to a secure attachment. A big shift for

Maisie was realising that she was in control now and responsible for her current behaviours. She started changing her habits, working with a coach and through therapy, she became more consciously aware. She now seeks out much healthier relationships and has achieved a more secure attachment type.

As we conclude this chapter, take a moment to contemplate how your attachment style impacts you.

- What have you learned?
- How are you going to implement this?

Chapter 2

Healing Towards a Secure Attachment

Taking a self-assessment or quiz on attachment styles can be a useful starting point for self-discovery and personal growth. These resources can offer guidance, insights and strategies for developing healthier attachment patterns and improving the quality of your relationships.

The good news is that attachment styles are not set in stone and with self-awareness, effort and often with the support of therapy or self-help resources, individuals with insecure attachment styles can work towards developing a more secure attachment style.

In this book, I will mostly concentrate on avoidant and anxious attachment styles as my focus is predominantly on families where trauma has not been present. However, it is important to acknowledge that individuals with a disorganised attachment type will also find the information relevant as a disorganised attachment will encompass aspects of both avoidant and anxious attachment styles.

By understanding the dynamics of your attachment style and learning strategies for developing more secure attachments, you will experience more fulfilling and healthy relationships, improved emotional well-being and personal growth. The journey towards secure attachment is indeed achievable and can lead to positive transformations in your life.

Personally, I once grappled with an anxious attachment style. I was persistently plagued by the fear that my friends or romantic partners would lose interest in me and vanish from my life. Moreover, I carried the unwarranted burden of believing that if such a scenario unfolded, it would be entirely my fault. My self-esteem was at a low ebb, I constantly felt like a failure in life and was convinced that everyone else was outperforming me. This often translated into feelings of jealousy and suspicion in my relationships, as I harboured anxieties that my partners might betray me or abandon me.

I employed the methods I'm about to explain, alongside therapy, to establish a secure attachment. By enhancing my self-esteem and self-value, I've successfully nurtured positive connections, both in my relationships with others and within myself.

Managing Anxiety in the Moment

Before embarking on a journey to change your attachment style or work on anything I talk about in this book, it's crucial to learn how to manage anxiety in the present moment. Here are strategies to help you manage anxiety:

Breathing Exercises

- **Box Breathing** - Breathe in for four seconds, hold the breath for four seconds, breathe out for four seconds and hold for another four seconds.
- **Resonant Breathing** - Inhale for a count of five, then exhale for a count of five and keep repeating for a few minutes.
- **Pursed Lip Breathing** - Relax your neck and shoulders and, keeping your mouth closed, inhale slowly through the nose for three counts. Then, pucker or purse your lips as though you were going to whistle and exhale slowly by blowing air through your pursed lips for a count of four.

Breaking the State

When you're feeling anxious, you can break the state in a number of different ways, but predominantly through movement. Some examples are going for a walk, doing star jumps, going to the gym or for a bike ride or even doing yoga poses.

Grounding Activities

- **Reorientation** – Look around your environment. Use all of your senses and name five things you can see, five things you can hear, five things you can smell, and five things you can feel. Repeat by naming four of each and continue with three, then two then one.
- **Press Your Feet into the Ground** – Press your heels down into the ground, then press your toes into the floor ensuring equal pressure throughout your feet. Feel how your feet connect with the ground.
- **Grounding Objects** – Carry a small object with you that you can touch or hold when you feel anxious. The physical connection can provide comfort and a sense of security.
- **Positive Self-Talk and Self-Compassion** – Challenge negative thoughts and replace them with positive affirmations. Remind yourself that you are safe and capable of handling challenging situations. Treat yourself with kindness and compassion and acknowledge that it's ok to feel anxious and that you're doing your best.

Meditation and Mindfulness

Meditation

Meditation brings a myriad of benefits, promoting both mental and physical well-being. By fostering awareness and mindfulness it helps to reduce stress, anxiety and overall emotional turbulence. Meditation contributes to better emotional regulation and a heightened sense of self-awareness, thus fostering a positive outlook on life.

To meditate, find a quiet space, sit or lie comfortably, and focus on your breath or a specific point of attention. Close your eyes, relax and let thoughts come and go without attachment. Maintain gentle awareness, returning to your chosen focal point when distractions arise. Start with short sessions and gradually extend the duration as you become more comfortable. Regular practice, even for a few minutes each day, can cultivate mindfulness and promote mental well-being.

Mindfulness

Mindfulness is the practice of intentionally paying attention to the present moment without judgement. It involves being fully engaged in your thoughts, feelings and surroundings, bringing a heightened awareness of the here and now. By using mindfulness, you can develop a non-reactive and accepting mindset, reduce stress and promote a more balanced and centred approach to daily life.

Similar to meditation, allocate a few minutes to sit comfortably in a quiet space. Focus on your breath, observing each inhale and exhale without judgment. Alternatively, direct your attention to a specific sensation, like the feeling of your footsteps or the warmth of sunlight. When thoughts arise, acknowledge them without getting caught up and gently return your focus to the present moment. Consistent, brief mindfulness sessions can gradually enhance awareness and bring a sense of calm to your daily life.

By practising these strategies, you can better manage anxiety in the moment, which is a crucial step in working towards changing your attachment style and developing healthier, more secure relationships.

Healing Anxious Attachment

As you now know, attachment styles are a reflection of a learned pattern of behaviour. Once you can deal with your anxiety in the moment, the first step towards changing your attachment type is by becoming aware of the patterns. This includes:

Journalling

Journalling is a powerful and introspective tool that I will talk about throughout this book. It helps improve self-awareness and allows you to reflect on your thoughts, emotions and past experiences related to attachment.

Here are additional tips on effectively using journalling:

- **Consistency** – Make journalling a regular practice. Setting aside a specific time each day or week to journal can help you stay committed to the process.

- **Honesty** - Be honest. Journalling is a safe space for self-reflection so don't hold back on your thoughts and feelings.
- **Reflect on Triggers** - When you experience insecurity or heightened anxiety, particularly in relationships, write about the triggers or situations and explore why they made you feel the way they did.
- **Explore Childhood Experiences** - Reflect on your early childhood experiences and relationships with caregivers. Consider how these experiences have shaped your attachment style.
- **Track Progress** - As you work on healing and changing your attachment style, use your journal to track your progress. Celebrate small victories and note any positive changes in your relationships.
- **Seek Clarity** - Use journalling to gain clarity on what a healthy relationship means to you and what you need from others. This can guide your efforts in creating healthier attachments.
- **Self-Compassion** - Be gentle with yourself in your journalling process. Acknowledge any challenges or setbacks you encounter along the way and practice self-compassion.
- **Set Goals** - Consider setting specific goals related to healing your anxious attachment. Write down actionable steps.

journal

The following prompts will help you to explore and understand anxious attachment patterns:

- What are your biggest fears in relationships?
- Do you feel safe in your relationship?
- What is the healthiest relationship you have in your life right now?
- Which relationships do you feel secure in?
- What does a healthy relationship mean to you?
- What do you need most right now from the people in your life?
- How can you create healthier attachments with the people around you?
- What behaviours create positive and negative feelings within your relationships?

You can use journalling to record your attachments with significant others and how they've made you feel.

Control

Relationships, whether they are romantic, friendships or with family, become healthier, when you let go of the need to be in control all of the time. It is important to remember that you can only control yourself and that you have no control over others.

- **Healthy Boundaries** - Allow others the autonomy to make their own choices and respect their boundaries, this will help to build trust and foster healthier relationships.
- **Mutual Respect** - Recognising that everyone in a relationship has their own agency is a cornerstone of mutual respect. Trust others to make their own decisions.
- **Effective Communication** - Focus on open and honest communication. Express your needs, concerns and desires, whilst actively listening to others.
- **Problem-Solving** - Shift your mindset away from control and when faced with challenges, move towards problem-solving. Collaborate with others to find a solution that works for everyone involved.
- **Acceptance** - Understand that there are certain things you cannot control, such as other people's thoughts, feelings and actions. Learning to accept these limitations can reduce stress and anxiety in relationships.

- **Self-Control** - While you can't control others, you can control your own actions and reactions. Practice self-control and emotional regulation to respond to situations healthily and constructively.
- **Flexibility** - Be flexible in your expectations and open to compromise. A rigid need for control can lead to conflict.

Remember that letting go of control, doesn't mean giving up on your needs or values or giving away your power, quite the contrary; eliminating the need for control takes your power back. It's about finding a balance between asserting yourself and respecting others' autonomy. By focusing on what you can control - your own behaviours, choices and responses - you can create a healthier environment in your relationships.

Healthy Relationships

Reaching a balance in your relationships will improve your ability to use compromise and negotiation rationally. Finding a middle ground and working together as a team can help to resolve conflict and build a strong foundation of trust. Spending quality time together will strengthen bonds.

Allowing trust to grow and working together as a team, will strengthen your relationship. Communication is key to a healthy relationship. Honest and open communication allows for the expression of needs, concerns and feelings in a safe and supportive environment. It takes time and consistency to build trust, so be patient and reliable in your interactions.

Self-awareness is crucial in maintaining healthy relationships, it allows you to recognise and manage your own emotions which, in turn, helps you approach interactions with others more constructively.

Focus on the strengths in your relationships and show gratitude and appreciation. Simple acts of kindness and acknowledgement can go a long way in nurturing relationships. A great way to keep anxiety or insecurity at bay is to create positive affirmations based on the strengths and positive aspects of your relationship. These affirmations can serve as a reminder of the value within your connections. For example, "This friendship is a safe space" or "My relationship with x makes me feel calm".

Empathy involves understanding and validating the emotions of others. It creates a sense of emotional connection and support. It is important to nurture empathy within your relationships.

Healing Avoidant Attachment

Again, one of the first steps to healing an avoidant attachment is self-awareness and awareness of your patterns in behaviour. Engaging in self-exploration to understand the origins of your attachment type and reflecting on past experiences will help you to understand what has contributed.

journal

Journal prompts that might help you to understand your avoidant attachment are:

- What are the things you fear most in a relationship/friendship?
- When did you first start to feel emotionally distant from others?
- What experiences in your life have led to your avoidant attachment patterns?
- What do you believe to be the benefits of emotional detachment?
- What negative beliefs do you hold about relationships?
- How has your avoidance of vulnerability impacted your connections with others?
- What does emotional safety mean to you?
- What are strategies you can use to build trust?

Expression

If you are someone who avoids or blocks off their emotions, beginning to practice emotional awareness will be beneficial for you. Spend time reflecting on your feelings and try to name them. Be kind to yourself through this process and recognise that it is okay to feel, and that vulnerability is a strength, not a weakness. Start sharing your emotions (using 'I' statements to take ownership) in low-stakes situations with people you trust, and gradually build up to more significant conversations.

Cultivate active listening skills to better understand the emotions of others. This can garner more meaningful connections. Being aware of your body language and making small adjustments can signal to others that you're more open to connection. Try to make eye contact, uncross your arms and keep your head up - you could be pushing people away without even realising it. Start noticing non-verbal cues in others too, which will help you to recognise your own. Even ask for feedback from trusted friends or family members about your communication and expression. They can provide insight and support your growth.

Trust

Being able to trust is a fundamental step in overcoming an avoidant attachment style. It's a gradual process but will lead to more secure and fulfilling relationships.

Begin by reflecting on any past experiences or events that have contributed to your difficulty in trusting others. Understanding the origin of your trust issues can be empowering.

Start learning about other people. Get to know the people in your life, deepen the relationships and hopefully, you'll find that they are trustworthy. Through this, challenge your negative assumptions about trust; instead of assuming that people are untrustworthy, try to approach new relationships and interactions with a more neutral or positive mindset. Start by opening up about smaller things, gauge how others respond and build confidence in their trustworthiness gradually. Collect this as evidence to prove that not everyone is untrustworthy. Add to this evidence by noticing consistency. Trust develops when you observe reliable behaviour.

Forgiveness is an important facet of healing. If you've experienced past betrayals or disappointments, work on forgiving those who've harmed your trust. This isn't about excusing poor behaviour, but rather letting go of difficult emotions for your own wellbeing.

How to Forgive: Forgiveness starts with a willingness to let go of negative emotions; you can approach it through the following:

- **Acknowledge the Pain** - Recognise and accept the pain caused
- **Seek Understanding** - Try to understand the perspective of the person who hurt you

- **Release Resentment** - Consciously let go of feelings of anger, resentment and any desire for revenge
- **Practice Empathy** - Recognise the humanity and imperfections of the person who hurt you
- **Let Go of Control** - Accept that you can't change the past and instead focus on what you can control
- **Establish Boundaries** - To protect you in the future, whilst allowing room for forgiveness
- **Seek Support** - This can help you to gain perspective
- **Practice Self-Compassion** - Be gentle with yourself. Recognise that healing takes time
- **Choose Peace** - Ultimately, forgiveness is the choice to prioritise inner peace and emotional well-being over holding onto grudges

Healing Disorganised Attachment

Journalling

Understanding the triggers and reactions associated with disorganised attachment is a valuable first step in the healing process. Again, journalling can be a powerful tool for gaining insight into your emotional patterns and behaviours and because the very nature of disorganised attachment encompasses both anxious and avoidant types, you can use all of the prompts previously provided.

Another way in which you can use journalling is to start by listing situations or experiences that trigger strong emotional responses or discomfort in your relationships, being as specific as possible. Then, reflect on how these triggers make you feel. What emotions do they bring up when you encounter them and are there patterns in your emotional responses? Describe how you react when you're triggered and how these reactions impact your relationships. Reflect on how you can create a sense of safety in your relationships, both with yourself and others. What strategies can you employ to feel safe when triggered?

Be Kind to Yourself

Recognising and affirming the influence of your early life experience on your emotional well-being represents a pivotal stride toward healing. Equally significant is cultivating supportive relationships with friends or family members who understand your background and honour your boundaries.

Carving out moments for activities that bring you joy and embracing self-compassion are vital facets of self-care that foster a stronger sense of self-worth.

Practising kindness towards yourself entails challenging negative self-talk and replacing those detrimental self-beliefs with affirmations that radiate positivity. It includes keeping promises to yourself.

A fundamental element of constructing healthy relationships is the establishment of robust boundaries, coupled with clear and assertive communication of your needs.

It's important to acknowledge that healing from disorganised attachment is a gradual process that benefits from therapeutic support. Therefore, extend to yourself the virtues of kindness and patience through this transformative journey.

Emotional Regulation

The ultimate objective in addressing disorganised attachment is achieving emotional regulation. Here are strategies that can assist in this process:

- Acknowledge the influence of your attachment style
- Develop the practice of effectively communicating your emotions
- Allow yourself personal space when necessary
- Dedicate time to contemplate your needs

It's possible for all of us to heal our attachment styles and progress towards security. Commencing this journey with self-awareness is a promising starting point.

As we conclude this chapter, take a moment to contemplate how your attachment style impacts you and how you can advance towards a secure attachment type.

- What have you learned?
- How are you going to implement this?

Chapter 3

Schema Therapy – Part One

Expanding on the insights from Chapter One, let's delve into schema therapy. Developed by Jeffery Young, schema therapy involves examining organised patterns of thought and behaviour. In the context of Cognitive Behavioural Therapy (CBT), a schema represents a fundamental, deep-rooted belief held about yourself which is intricately linked to a network of memories, emotions and physical sensations. These schemas form during childhood and continue to evolve throughout your lifetime, manifesting as beliefs about yourself or the world. Deeply ingrained in our thought processes, these core beliefs significantly influence our perception of reality and serve as the foundational source of our negative automatic thoughts. Negative Automatic Thoughts, or NATs, are spontaneous thoughts that often arise in response to specific triggers. These thoughts are likely to be negative, self-critical and distorted. They influence emotions and behaviour.

Jeffery Young suggested that five emotional needs must be fulfilled during childhood:

1. **Connection/attachment** - Establishing secure bonds with others, encompassing feelings of safety, stability, nurturance, and acceptance.
2. **Autonomy** - Developing a sense of identity and competence.
3. **Freedom** - Encompasses the ability to express valid needs and emotions openly.
4. **Flow** - The capacity for spontaneity and play.
5. **Boundaries** - Establishing realistic limits and acquiring self-control skills.

As a child progresses through their developmental stages, they rely on parents or caregivers to fulfil their emotional needs. However, given the human nature of all of our parents and caregivers, they occasionally fall short, significantly influencing our developmental trajectory.

Three types of coping mechanisms exist for managing schema which, rather than effectively addressing them, typically end up reinforcing these patterns.

- **Avoidance** - Steering clear of situations that trigger the schema or belief.
- **Surrender** - Yielding to the schema without resisting, anticipating an inevitable outcome.
- **Overcompensation** - Investing additional effort to prevent the perceived outcome from occurring.

What are the eighteen Schemas as defined by Jeffery Young? And how can we start to heal them?

1. Abandonment

If you have this schema, you anticipate a lack of consistent support, connection or protection from others. You perceive relationships as generally unstable, unreliable or unpredictable, leading to a belief that abandonment is imminent or inevitable when in a relationship.

The Origin of the Abandonment Schema

This schema typically emerges during childhood as a result of an unfulfilled requirement for consistent support, connection and protection. Various factors contribute to this unmet need, such as a primary caregiver being unresponsive to the child's needs, misinterpretation of those needs, or the caregiver's own mental health issues. Actual instances of abandonment, extended periods of separation due to a parent working away, or the loss of a primary caregiver through death can also give rise to the development of this schema.

Recognising the Presence of an Abandonment Schema

Signs of the abandonment schema are:

- Concern that others will leave you, either unintentionally or through choice
- Hypervigilance about signs of desertion
- Monitoring surroundings and loved ones for signs of withdrawal of support or connection
- Worry about others leaving
- Becoming clingy, jealous or controlling
- Seeking out a lot of reassurance within your relationships
- Being obsessive within relationships and finding focussing on other things difficult
- Low self-worth, feeling that your needs weren't met because you were undeserving
- People pleasing
- General stress and anxiety
- Unhealthy coping strategies

HEALING YOUR ABANDONMENT SCHEMA

Disrupting Patterns

Frequently, we attract individuals to us who reinforce our schemas. Reflect on whether those around you contribute to your sense of abandonment. Opt to surround yourself with those who foster your feelings of safety and understanding.

Additionally, consider engaging in inner child work, a topic we'll explore in a subsequent chapter. This practice helps cultivate a compassionate, nurturing adult aspect of yourself that attends to the vulnerable, younger parts within.

Practice Rationalisation, Not Catastrophisation

When interpreting the behaviours of others, we often construct narratives or hypothetical scenarios. It's crucial to be aware of whether you tend to immediately gravitate towards the worst-case scenario in these stories. For instance, if your partner doesn't promptly respond to a text message, someone with an abandonment schema might automatically assume they are leaving or losing interest when in reality, they could have been busy with work or in a meeting.

Strive to extend the benefit of the doubt to those close to you when their actions deviate from your expectations. Remind yourself that your thoughts do not necessarily equate to reality. If there is a fear of others leaving, try to find evidence to counteract these fears.

Incorporating meditation or mindfulness practices can assist in staying present and letting go of intrusive thoughts and emotions.

Self-Awareness

Self-awareness is a crucial element in addressing the wounds of abandonment. Take time to contemplate how this pattern has influenced your life and consider its origins. Identify your triggers and observe your emotional responses and subsequent reactions when triggered.

journal

Journal prompts for healing the abandonment schema are:

- As a child, did you feel supported and loved? What did your caregivers provide you or not provide you with emotionally?
- Did you feel safe and secure as a child?
- How do you view and understand love? What does love mean to you?
- Have you felt abandoned by a significant person in your life? How has this impacted your ability to trust?
- Are there any recurring patterns in your relationships? How do they manifest? And what impact do they have on your emotions?
- Can you recognise any unhealthy coping mechanisms you've developed to deal with abandonment issues? How do these mechanisms impact on you and your relationships?
- Explore instances where you have pushed people away. What can you learn from these experiences?

2. Mistrust/Abuse

If you have this schema, you anticipate others mistreating you, perceiving them as untrustworthy. You anticipate dishonesty, manipulation, exploitation or even harm from others.

The Origin of the Mistrust/Abuse Schema

In this context, it can be assumed that caregivers have purposefully neglected their child's needs and signals. This can be a result of the caregivers having experienced similar neglect or abuse in their past and are now perpetuating this cycle with their offspring. Alternatively, they lack the internal resources to adequately meet their child's needs, for example, they may be struggling with mental health issues.

How Might You Know if You Have a Mistrust/Abuse Schema?

The impacts of this schema can be severe and varied and go hand in hand with a disorganised attachment type. They can be difficult to recognise, however, signs include:

- Constant concerns about being mistreated by others
- Feeling withdrawn and anxious
- Have few friends and avoiding relationships

- Act physically or verbally aggressive to others to assert control
- Suspicious of authority figures
- Difficulty trusting
- Feeling you are taken advantage of more than others
- Hypervigilant to mistreatment (appear suspicious)
- Unhealthy coping mechanisms

HEALING YOUR MISTRUST/ABUSE SCHEMA

Embrace the Present

Reaffirm your control over your present life; there is no obligation to persist in the behaviours from your childhood. While challenging when triggered, use meditation and mindfulness to anchor yourself in the current moment. Train your mind to concentrate on the present and allow other thoughts and emotions to dissipate.

Your Circle

Evaluate if those around you are validating your trust-related beliefs; choose to be in the company of individuals who treat you positively. Exercise judgement, by taking small risks in confiding things to people and when trust is proven, recall these minor triumphs and accumulate evidence to reinforce the notion that people around you are indeed reliable and trustworthy.

journal

Reflect on your trust issues and the specific areas where you struggle, identifying your triggers and patterns. Prompts you can journal on are:

- What experiences have affected your ability to trust? Are there themes or patterns within this?
- How do trust issues manifest in your relationships?
- What fears contribute to your lack of trust?
- What situations or behaviours trigger your trust issues?
- How do you respond when your trust is challenged?
- How has your past experience impacted on beliefs and expectations around trust?
- What emotions arise when you think about trusting others?
- How might your life improve if you trust more fully?

3. Emotional Deprivation

If you sense a lack of emotional connections with others and experience a sense of emptiness, you might be dealing with an emotional deprivation schema. This schema implies an anticipation that your requirements for care, empathy and protection will never be completely fulfilled, resulting in feelings of loneliness and a lack of support.

The Origin of the Emotional Deprivation Schema

This schema emerges during childhood when the caregiver fails to align with the child's needs, either by overlooking their cues or interpreting them inaccurately. Alternatively, the caregiver may recognise the child's needs but lack the internal resources to address them due to mental health issues or their own schemas. Despite the caregivers' good intentions, the child still perceives a shortfall in having their emotional needs fulfilled.

How Might You Know if You Have an Emotional Deprivation Schema?

There are three different forms of emotional deprivation:

- Not being given love, affection or nurturing
- Being deprived of empathy
- Not having anyone to rely on for support

The signs to look out for to recognise this schema are:

- Feelings of loneliness, depression or anxiety
- Believing your wants and needs are unimportant and not communicating them
- Feeling alone or empty
- Feeling secondary or less important than others
- Acting tougher than you are
- Possibly avoiding relationships or avoiding having your needs unmet[HH2]
- Conversely, being clingy or over-expressing your needs
- Attraction to people who are incapable of meeting your needs

HEALING YOUR EMOTIONAL DEPRIVATION SCHEMA

Evaluate Your Expectations

Prolonged unmet emotional needs leads to expectations that exceed what others can genuinely provide. Recognise that individuals typically aren't withholding affection, empathy or protection; they are offering what they can when they can. Whenever possible choose to be around individuals who contribute to making you feel loved and secure.

Embrace Vulnerability

Allow yourself to feel your emotions without suppressing or dismissing them, as you have learned to do. Acknowledge that facing your emotions demonstrates courage rather than weakness. Endeavour to be more transparent and open with those in your life.

journal

Journal prompts that might help with this schema are:

- Which emotions are you trying to avoid?
- Why are you trying to hide from this emotion?
- What is preventing you from addressing this feeling?
- How did you receive love as a child?
- What does love mean for you?
- What are your needs from this relationship? How will you know if they are being met?
- How does expressing your emotions make you feel?

4. Defectiveness/Shame

Possessing this schema implies a sense that there is a flaw within you. This perceived imperfection can apply to various aspects, such as appearance, personality, values, intelligence and more. Holding on to the belief of having this flaw includes feelings of shame and fosters the fear that as others come to know you better, they will uncover this defect, ultimately resulting in rejection.

The Origin of the Defectiveness/Shame Schema

For this schema to develop, the caregiver might express criticism towards their child either verbally or through their behaviour. This tendency could stem from the caregiver's own exposure to this form of parenting.

How Might You Know if You Have a Defectiveness/Shame Schema?

Signs of this schema are:

- Belief that others will reject you because you are flawed
- Belief that you would be more lovable or acceptable if you were different
- Self-conscious or passive in interactions with others
- Seeking reassurance and approval from others

- Withdrawn and anxious about others or aggressive towards others
- Hypersensitivity to rejection, criticism, blame or comparison
- Self-critical and devaluing your successes and positive qualities
- Sense of shame or embarrassment
- Fear of your flaws being exposed
- Stress and unhealthy coping mechanisms
- Avoiding relationships or jumping from one to another

HEALING YOUR DEFECTIVENESS/SHAME SCHEMA

Work Out How it Influences You

This might not affect every aspect of your life; for instance, you may only feel inadequate at work or in certain friendships. To effectively address it, identify the specific situations that trigger these feelings and focus on them.

Cease Comparisons

People typically present themselves in a way they desire, particularly on social media but in lots of other aspects too. Consider restricting your access to social media and unfollowing those who prompt unfavourable comparisons and lead to you feeling inadequate. Work to only be a better version of yourself in order to take your focus away from others.

Cultivate gratitude for the positive aspects of your life. Make a daily habit of listing something you are thankful for, even if it's a small thing like a sunny day or a beautiful sunset. With this routine, you'll become more attuned to the positive aspects of your life.

Self-Love

Recognise that every single one of us deserves love and respect, irrespective of perceived flaws or imperfections. Understand that you adopted this belief during childhood and acknowledge that you have evolved beyond this phase. Remember to speak to yourself as you would a friend, employing compassion and generosity.

Create a list of your positive attributes, even if it's just one per day, however tiny and refer to this list when your feelings of defectiveness or shame are triggered. Look for the things you do well, even if it's small things like cooking a nice meal or a small act of kindness, this will shift your focus away from your perceived flaws.

journal

Journal prompts that might help with this schema are:

- When did you first feel defective or shamed?
- What other perspectives can you look at your childhood experience from?
- When do feelings of shame get triggered?
- How can you manage healthy boundaries?
- How can you be more vulnerable with people?
- When you feel shame, how do you react (e.g., eat, get angry, blame someone)?
- What are the negative thoughts you have about yourself that are rooted in shame?
- Write a letter to your younger self, expressing compassion and understanding for the things that have caused you shame.

5. Social Isolation

Those of you harbouring this schema experience a sense of not fitting in anywhere. You perceive yourself as different and feel disconnected or alienated from others, leading you to actively avoid social situations.

The Origin of the Social Isolation Schema

This schema develops when a child is raised in a socially isolated family or perceives themselves as different from the mainstream. Various factors, such as exceptional intelligence, unconventional appearance, family background, sexual orientation, disability, religion or financial and social status, can contribute to this feeling of being different. Additionally, a child might feel distinct from their family, experiencing a sense of inadequacy or differentiation from their siblings.

How Might You Know if You Have a Social Isolation Schema?

Signs of the social isolation schema are:

- Feeling like you don't belong
- Avoiding people and feeling like relationships can be exhausting
- Feeling like you can only relax when you are alone
- Feeling like you have to hide who you are

- Feeling, deep down, that if people see the real you, they will reject you
- Comparing yourself and assuming that others are better than you
- Strong inner critic
- Telling yourself you prefer solitude at the same time as feeling lonely

HEALING YOUR SOCIAL ISOLATION SCHEMA

Reflect on the Past

Seek to understand where you received the message that you are somehow different. Was it influenced by the way you were treated by parents and siblings or was it experiences at school? Strive to examine this objectively, as if observing someone else's life. Question whether it is justified for someone to be treated in this manner. Recognise that you may not be as distinct from others as you perceive and compile a list of qualities you share with them.

Establish Connections

In order to establish connections recognise the negative thoughts that deter you from participating in groups or forming connections. Seek evidence both supporting and refuting these thoughts. Incrementally increase your time spent with people, actively initiating conversations and staying grounded throughout the process.

Endeavour to become a part of something larger than yourself, such as engaging in community activities or volunteering. Take small steps towards making new friends.

journal

Journal prompts to help with social isolation schema:

- How do you feel about your current level of social interaction?
- Are there any past experiences or events that have led to you feeling socially isolated?
- What social and emotional needs are currently unmet in your life?
- How can you prioritise these needs moving forwards?
- Who are the people in your life who provide support?
- How can you strengthen or nurture these relationships?
- What steps can you take to reintegrate into social activities or groups?
- Do you have any interests or hobbies?
- What specific social goals would you like to achieve? And how can you break them down in to achievable steps?

6. Dependence/Incompetence

Those of you with this schema feel like you can't always cope, like you can't make decisions on your own or that tasks are too difficult for you.

The Origin of the Dependence/Incompetence Schema

Commonly associated with this schema is a childhood where caregivers display excessive protectiveness. In such cases, children are shielded from life's challenges, fostering fears about handling routine situations. Caregivers might continue to perform tasks for the child even when they are capable of doing them independently, inadvertently instilling the belief that the child lacks the capability to perform tasks on their own.

Alternatively, this schema emerges if a child experiences neglect, attempting skills and facing failure alone, with no guidance, reinforcing the belief that they are incapable.

How Might You Know If You Have a Dependence/Incompetence Schema?

Signs that you might recognise if you have the dependence/incompetence schema are:

- Feeling helpless or fearful or unable to cope with day-to-day life
- Worry when left without help
- Gravitate towards others who are more confident (potentially reinforcing the belief that you are incompetent)
- Doubting own judgement and ability to perform tasks competently
- Ask for advice or guidance repeatedly before making decisions
- Reluctance to live independently
- Highly self-critical - feeling that you are a failure
- Worry that you are a burden to loved ones
- Refuse opportunities for increased responsibility or growth
- Avoidance of trying, due to the belief that you'll not be able to do things

HEALING YOUR DEPENDENCE/INCOMPETENCE SCHEMA

Step Beyond Self Doubt

Whilst occasional questioning of your judgement is natural, it's crucial to be aware if you tend to believe that you will consistently make incorrect decisions. Grant yourself the room to acknowledge that this view is not an accurate reflection of the current situation. Practices such as meditation or mindfulness can effectively train your attention to focus on the present and release extraneous thoughts and feelings. Acknowledge that you extend beyond your perceived shortcomings. Compile a list of instances when you achieved desired outcomes through your actions (no accomplishment is too small) and turn to this list when your schema is triggered.

Be Mindful of How Much You Let Others Do

Take note of the extent to which you rely on others. Are you letting them handle tasks that you should be doing yourself? Do you defer your decisions to others or consistently seek advice to avoid making decisions independently? Reflect on whether those closest to you inadvertently reinforce your schema. Pose these questions to yourself and implement changes where needed. Surround yourself with people who respect you and treat you well. Communicate your desire to take steps towards greater independence from those around you, seeking their support and allowing space for your personal growth.

Build Your Confidence

Start the process by creating a list of tasks you aspire to achieve independently. Organise them from the simplest to the most challenging. Begin with the easiest task, break it down into smaller components and commence with the initial steps, completing each one. As you accomplish these tasks, your self-confidence will naturally strengthen.

Acknowledging that taking on new tasks inevitably involves making a few mistakes is vital. Understand that making mistakes doesn't equate to incompetence. Accept the consequences of the errors, remind yourself of your capability to address them and use the experience to foster personal growth.

journal

Journal prompts to help with the Dependence/Incompetence schema are:

- What thoughts or beliefs make you feel dependent or incompetent in certain situations?
- Reflect on your childhood experiences. Where there any events or dynamics that have contributed to feelings of dependence?
- List your strengths and abilities. What are your unique qualities that counteract feelings of incompetence?
- Recall instances where you demonstrated self-reliance or competence?
- Who are the people in your life who offer support and encouragement? How do they empower you?
- How do you aspire to greater independence?

How will independence enrich your life?

7. Vulnerability to Harm/Illness

Those of you with this schema may often worry that something terrible is going to happen, or fear that the world is unsafe for you and your family. There may also be a fear of illness disproportionate to what is going on in your body.

There are three areas that this schema can be split into: **Medical** (fear of illnesses such as cancer or heart attacks), **Emotional** (fear of panic attacks or being admitted for psychiatric help) and **External** (fear of natural disasters, being a victim of crime etc.)

The Origin of the Vulnerability to Harm/Illness Schema

Once more, this schema commonly emerges when caregivers exhibit excessive protectiveness and heightened concerns about the child's safety. Caregivers employ exaggerated language to excessively caution their child about potential dangers, fostering the belief that the world is in inherently perilous place which demands constant caution. Additionally, this schema can develop in the aftermath of a traumatic experience, such as the loss of a loved one, abuse or encountering injury or illness.

How Might You Know if You Have a Vulnerability To Harm/Illness Schema?

Signs of this schema that you might recognise are:

- Disproportionate level of fear about bad things that happen
- Relying on others a lot for reassurance
- Feeling isolated, like others don't understand your worries.
- Difficulty concentrating on day-to-day tasks
- Restricting your access to various activities
- Difficulty sleeping
- Chronic stress due to hypervigilance

HEALING YOUR VULNERABILITY TO HARM/ILLNESS SCHEMA

Mindfulness

Start by identifying the specific concerns that occupy your thoughts, such as fears of crime or attacks. Maintain a record of when these thoughts come up, identify triggers and note any recurring patterns. Employ techniques as discussed in the previous chapter, like breathing exercises, muscle relaxation and grounding to alleviate anxiety and anchor yourself in the present moment. Training your mind in these practices facilitates releasing the grip of past concerns.

It's crucial to recognise that fears stemming from vulnerability to harm or illness don't align with reality. Be mindful of any inclination to immediately jump to worst-case scenarios and actively challenge these thoughts as they arise.

Gather Supporting Evidence

Seek out evidence that contradicts your fears and assess the realistic likelihood of their occurrence. Document instances when things have gone well and maintain a list to refer to when triggered. For instance, if you fear flying, record how frequently negative incidents have happened during flights. Continuously practice this shift in mindset to become more aware of anxious thoughts, redirecting them as needed. Consistently ask yourself - *What else could be true?*

Minimise the Need for Reassurance

Individuals with this schema often find themselves seeking reassurance and although this provides temporary relief, it fails to tackle the core issue. Moreover, it can transform into a compulsive behaviour, placing a burden on those from whom reassurance is sought. When the urge for reassurance arises, attempt to find it within yourself. Evaluate the realism of your worries and concentrate on the present moment. When feelings of helplessness surface, remember to interrupt your thought pattern by actively recounting all the ways in which you independently provide for yourself, utilising your strengths to address challenges.

journal

Journal prompts to help with this schema are:

- What specific concerns or fears are currently on your mind?
- Reflect on the origins of each fear. Are there past experiences that contribute to it?
- How do you cope with feelings of vulnerability to harm or illness?
- What self-care do you use to maintain physical and emotional well-being?
- List three things about your health that you are grateful for today.
- What affirmations can you use to promote feelings of safety, health, and well-being?

8. Enmeshment/Under-Developed Self

Those of you with this schema might experience a sense that your life isn't entirely self-defined and find it challenging to articulate your identity without referencing another person.

The Origin of the Enmeshment/Under-Developed Self Schema

This schema develops when caregivers discourage the child from expressing their unique needs, thoughts and emotions. The child might have been subtly led to believe that having divergent thoughts and emotions is wrong, inducing feelings of guilt for experiencing them. This can lead the child to the belief that acceptance hinges on aligning their emotions and beliefs with those of the caregivers. Alternatively, the child might have been made to feel responsible for the caregiver's needs and emotions. For instance, if the caregiver was upset, they will have attributed these feelings to the child's behaviour, instilling a sense of guilt or shame in the child.

How Might You Know if You Have an Enmeshment/Under-Developed Self Schema?

Signs of this schema are:

- Seeing yourself as an extension of another person
- Finding it difficult to socialise
- Feeling extreme emotional connection and intimacy to the detriment of your own self-identity
- Difficulty being yourself
- Copying behaviours of the person you're enmeshed with
- Suppressing any independent thoughts or behaviours
- Experiencing clinginess and hypersensitivity to rejection
- Having no sense of who you are outside of another person
- Feeling directionless and empty
- Poor decision making
- Feeling trapped and guilty

HEALING YOUR ENMESHMENT/UNDERDEVELOPED-SELF SCHEMA

Define Your Individuality

Initiate the process of establishing a distinct identity by creating a list outlining the advantages of having a separate identity from another person. Keep this list handy for reference during triggering moments. Assess the degree of differentiation from the person with whom you feel enmeshed. Begin by identifying similarities and differences, acknowledging that each small dissimilarity serves as evidence of your unique individuality.

Next, explore your preferences independently of the other person. Start with minor choices, such as your preference for tea or coffee, and gradually progress to more significant aspects, like your needs and wants. Pose questions to yourself, delving into your values and desires: What holds importance for you? What is necessary for your contentment? This process helps you affirm and understand your personal identity outside of external influences.

Cultivate Contentment in Your Own Company

Strive to foster a positive relationship with yourself and embrace solitude. Visualise engaging in activities without the presence of others and savouring them without any lingering guilt or discomfort. Progress gradually, starting with smaller endeavours, such as watching a movie at home alone and gradually working your way up to more substantial activities, such as going to an event or for a walk alone. If anxiety becomes a hurdle, consider practising meditation or mindfulness to anchor yourself in the present moment.

Establish Personal Limits

In the context of this schema, setting and maintaining boundaries becomes vital. In a healthy relationship, your boundaries should be honoured. For instance, you might establish a boundary of not responding to messages after nine pm. If someone contacts you beyond that time, you can uphold your boundary, by choosing not to respond. If questioned, reiterate your established boundary. Initially, you might experience feelings of guilt or discomfort, but with time, it will become more manageable. Holding firm to your boundaries is a vital way to avoid falling into another enmeshed relationship. Surround yourself with individuals who respect and treat you well, ensuring that connections with others never come at the expense of your own identity.

You can establish boundaries using the following method:

- **Self-reflection** – Take time to understand your needs, values and limits.
- **Identify boundaries** – Determine what is acceptable and unacceptable to you.
- **Communicate clearly** – Express your boundaries assertively, using I statements to convey your feelings without blame or criticism.
- **Enforce consistently** – Be firm in upholding boundaries, and assertive in addressing any violations.

journal

Journal prompts for this schema are:

- Reflect on specific situations or relationships where you feel enmeshed or unable to establish your own identity.
- Consider the origins of enmeshment in your life. Are there dynamics or past experiences that contribute to this pattern?
- Describe your current strategy for setting and maintaining boundaries.
- List your desires or aspirations that you have set aside or neglected due to enmeshment.
- What steps can you take to reclaim your independence?
- Who supports you to break free from enmeshment and encourages your self-development?
- What affirmations will help to emphasise your uniqueness?

9. Failure

Those of you with this schema often hold the belief that you have failed, will continue to fail, and are inherently inadequate when compared to others. Your self-perception tends to be highly negative, and you may consider yourself unintelligent or incompetent. I personally held this schema for many years prior to healing.

The Origin of the Failure Schema

Various childhood situations can contribute to the emergence of the failure schema. These involve caregivers subjecting the child to ridicule, mockery or criticism, setting unattainable expectations that the child cannot meet, inadequate discipline or support from caregivers and encounters with bullying or embarrassment in school or other social environments. For me, my mum always set the academic bar very high. This came about because she wasn't encouraged in this way and was left feeling that she hadn't met her potential. She didn't want that for me. These high standards, as well as embarrassing situations at primary school, unfortunately, led to comparing myself to others, developing a fear of failing or being unsuccessful and procrastinating, giving up on tasks and showing little progress at work, which perpetuated my fears.

How Might You Know if You Have a Failure Schema?

Signs of the failure schema are:

- Feeling incapable of success
- Having a sense of inferiority in comparison to others
- Lacking self-worth or feeling undeserving
- Procrastinating when dealing with important tasks
- Having a general lack of self-confidence
- Having a sense of shame about your progress
- Giving up on tasks quickly or avoiding tasks you perceive yourself as being bad at
- Getting frustrated or upset when you do something wrong
- Showing little progression in the workplace as you fear being unsuccessful
- Feeling stupid or incompetent
- Responding sensitively to feedback, focussing on the negatives
- Constantly comparing yourself to others

HEALING YOUR FAILURE SCHEMA

Acknowledge the Fear of Failure

Acknowledge the presence of your fear of failure and recognise that experiencing failure is a common aspect of the human journey and not indicative of weakness. Reflect on how this fear has influenced your life, decisions and goals. Begin to question the negative beliefs and thoughts that contribute to your fear of failure, such as self-criticism, perfectionism and all-or-nothing thinking. Gather evidence of instances when you haven't failed and assess whether there is substantial evidence supporting the self-critical thoughts - often, there isn't.

I started my healing journey by looking at the evidence I had that I'd failed. This was very limited and any failures that I did unearth were generally a direct result of procrastination, due to a fear of failure.

Reframe Failure

Comprehend that failure is not an enduring condition, but a transient setback. Instead of viewing it negatively, consider it as an opportunity for learning and growth. Embrace a growth mindset, which perceives challenges and failures as the chance to acquire new skills and evolve as an individual. Analyse the aspects that led to the setback and work out what can be approached differently in the future. Employ journalling as a tool to monitor your progress and reflect on your experiences. Enhance your resilience by rebounding from setbacks and recalling past successes as well as challenges you have successfully overcome. Personally, I now view failure as an opportunity to learn and grow.

Establish Achievable Goals

Break your overarching goals into smaller, more attainable steps to make the journey to success seem less overwhelming and alleviate the fear of failure. Start to become consciously aware of any avoidant activity such as procrastination and steer clear of this avoidance as it only enhances the fear of failure. Begin by taking small, manageable risks in the areas where you fear failure. Celebrate not just the final outcome, but your effort and progress along the way, including anything that you perceive as failure -it is not failure, it is a necessary step on the road to success.

Now, I set myself targets and break them down into achievable steps. I work on the steps, reducing overwhelm and the fear of the bigger task.

Practice Self-Compassion

Extend kindness to yourself. Keep in mind that nobody is perfect and mistakes are a universal part of being human. Treat yourself with the same empathy and understanding that you would offer to a friend facing a similar situation.

journal

Journal prompts that help with this schema are:

- What fears or doubts do you associate with failure?
- How have these fears held you back in the past?
- What negative beliefs or self-criticism come to mind when you think about failing?
- Can you trace the origins of these beliefs?
- How can you redefine failure more positively and constructively?
- What opportunities for learning and growth can you see in past failures?
- What are achievable, smaller steps that you can take towards your larger goals?
- How might breaking your goals into pieces make them less intimidating?
- How will you celebrate your efforts, regardless of the outcome?
- How do you typically treat yourself when you make a mistake or encounter failure?
- What can you say to yourself in those moments to show self-compassion?

As we conclude this chapter, take a moment to contemplate how your schemas impact you and how you can work towards minimalizing this impact.

- What have you learned?
- How are you going to implement this?

Chapter 4

Schema Therapy – Part Two

10. Entitlement/Grandiosity

Those of you with this schema experience a sense of being special, of feeling that you are better than others and thus entitled to special treatment and privileges. In relationships, you don't feel the need to reciprocate and might attempt to manipulate others to fulfil your needs.

The Origin of the Entitlement/Grandiosity Schema

There are two types within this schema:

- **Fragile or Narcissistic Entitlement:** this is when people overcompensate for the defectiveness schema and so, are actually compensating for feelings of shame and inadequacy.
- **Pure Entitlement:** This is when the parents have spoiled or over-indulged the child, for example,

by not setting limits or by allowing them to do what they wanted, thus embedding the belief that they are special.

How Might You Know if You Have an Entitlement/Grandiosity Schema?

Signs of this schema are:

- Finding it difficult to take no for an answer
- Feeling you shouldn't have to follow the normal rules of society
- Finding it difficult to admit you're wrong
- Putting yourself first/believing your own needs and wants are the most important
- Being controlling or domineering
- Finding it difficult to be told what to do
- Having little respect for authority
- Feeling superior to others
- Feeling you should be able to do what you want, when you want

HEALING YOUR ENTITLEMENT/GRANDIOSITY SCHEMA

Challenge Your Beliefs

Identify specific entitlement or grandiosity beliefs that you hold, such as the conviction that you deserve special treatment or possess inherent superiority. Scrutinise the evidence supporting these beliefs and assess whether they align with reality or if they are exaggerated. Reflect on how these beliefs have impacted your relationships and overall well-being.

Cultivate Humility and Empathy

Embrace the realisation that, like everyone else, you are not infallible and have inherent limitations. Appreciate the valuable contributions and diverse perspectives of those around you and foster a genuine openness to learning from them. Develop empathy by actively considering situations from others' viewpoints. Reflect on the impact of your actions and words and understand how others might feel as a result of them. Align your expectations with reality, recognising that special treatment or guaranteed success is not a given. If your sense of entitlement has caused harm to others, demonstrate sincerity by offering genuine apologies, taking responsibility for your actions and actively working to rectify any wrong doings. Such efforts can significantly contribute to relationship building.

Seek Constructive Feedback

Initiate a dialogue with friends, family or even your therapist to gain candid feedback regarding any perceived entitlement or grandiosity in your behaviour. Embrace their insights with an open mind and demonstrate a genuine willingness to implement changes based on their observations. Accept responsibility for your actions and their repercussions and refrain from placing blame on others or external factors for any mistakes or shortcomings. This proactive approach fosters personal growth and strengthens your commitment to constructive self-awareness.

Embrace the Present Moment

Incorporate mindfulness techniques to heighten awareness of your thoughts and behaviours in the present moment. Reflect on your actions and assess their alignment with your aspirations for change. Additionally cultivate gratitude for the positive aspects of your life, intentionally redirecting your focus from entitlement to a sincere appreciation for what you currently possess. This shift in perspective fosters a greater sense of mindfulness and contentment.

journal

Journal prompts that will help with this schema are:

- What does entitlement mean to you? And how do you define it in your own life?
- Can you recall specific situations where you felt entitled or acted in a grandiose manner?
- What are the core beliefs or thoughts that contribute to your sense of entitlement or grandiosity?
- How have these beliefs influenced your actions and interactions with others?
- Reflect on your relationships with friends, family or colleagues. In what way has your entitlement affected these relationships?
- Do you see any connections between your childhood and development of entitlement beliefs?
- List your entitlement beliefs and question their validity.
- How might challenging these beliefs lead to healthier perspectives and behaviours?
- What does humility mean to you?
- Can you recall moments when humility played a positive role in your life?

11. Insufficient Self-Control/Self-Discipline

Those with this schema experience heightened restlessness or boredom and encounter challenges in adhering to plans or goals. Additionally, they grapple with issues related to impulse control and find it difficult to resist immediate urges or desires.

The Origin of the Insufficient Self-Control/Self-Discipline Schema

The development of this schema is linked to an underdeveloped prefrontal cortex, which can occur when children are not taught discipline within a framework of rules and boundaries. In such cases, these children miss out on acquiring crucial skills, like practising patience and managing discomfort, due to the absence of necessary limits.

How Might You Know if You Have an Insufficient Self-Control/Self-Discipline Schema?

Signs of this schema are:

- Acting on impulse and feeling regret later
- Feeling restless or bored
- Engaging in self-sabotage behaviours such as drinking, smoking or over-eating
- Struggling to see tasks through to completion
- Avoiding uncomfortable feelings

- Chaotic emotions
- Procrastination
- Difficulty managing money

HEALING YOUR INSUFFICIENT SELF-CONTROL/ SELF-DISCIPLINE SCHEMA

Enhance Self-Awareness

Begin by comprehending the ways in which this schema is influencing your life, whether through procrastination, impulsivity or challenges in achieving goals. Identify the precise areas where self-discipline is lacking, be it in work, health, relationships or other aspects.

Establish clear objectives tailored to each identified area to provide a sense of purpose and direction. Develop a strategic plan to attain these goals by breaking them down into smaller, manageable steps. This structured approach enhances self-awareness and facilitates proactive efforts towards personal growth.

Cultivate Mindfulness

Engage in mindfulness techniques to heighten awareness of your impulses and reactions and foster improved self-control. Implement practices that involve delaying immediate gratification in favour of longer-term rewards, as this can serve as a potent strategy for enhancing your self-discipline.

Embrace Accountability

Confide in trusted friends or family members about your goals and enlist their support to hold you accountable for your actions. Simultaneously, focus on cultivating positive habits that contribute to self-discipline. Establishing consistency in your routines is instrumental in reinforcing these habits and promoting a more disciplined approach to your endeavours.

Elevate Self-Care

Make self-care a top priority to ensure you possess the necessary energy and focus for practising self-discipline. Eliminate sources of temptation that trigger impulsive behaviours to establish a more secure and conducive environment. Celebrate your achievements by rewarding yourself, thus reinforcing the desired behaviour. Acknowledge that setbacks are a natural part of the process and cultivate resilience to bounce back. Engage in compassionate self-talk and use setbacks as opportunities for reflection and learning.

journal

Journal prompts that help with this schema are:

- In what specific areas of your life do you struggle with self-control or self-discipline?
- How has lack of discipline impacted your goals and well-being?
- How can you break your goals into smaller, actionable steps?
- What situations or temptations tend to trigger your lack of self-control?
- How can you proactively avoid or manage these triggers?
- What self-care practices can you incorporate to maintain the energy or focus needed for self-control?
- What positive habits do you want to cultivate?
- What strategies have been most effective in improving your self-control?

12. Subjugation

Individuals with this schema perceive that their thoughts, feelings and needs hold little significance. They might yield to others to sidestep conflict, ultimately leading to a sense of resentment.

The Origin of the Subjugation Schema

This schema arises when children discover that asserting themselves is met with negative consequences such as punishment, humiliation or disregard. Consequently, they develop a fear of expressing their emotions.

Another pathway for the development of this schema involves feelings of guilt. In such cases, children have shouldered a sense of responsibility for the needs or emotions of their parent or caregiver, due to the caregiver's vulnerability or coercion. For instance, the child may have been raised to believe that having their own emotions was wrong.

This guilt can extend to saying no, driven by a fear of disappointing their caregiver and a tendency to suppress their emotions in a bid for approval.

How Might You Know If You Have a Subjugation Schema?

Signs of the subjugation schema are:

- Feeling that the needs and emotions of others are more important than your own
- Gravitating to those who appear more sure of themselves
- Having fear that if you voice your needs or emotions, you will disappoint someone
- Feelings of frustration or anger towards others
- Taking on more than your share of responsibility
- Feeling uncomfortable asking for help
- Feeling unable to protect your boundaries

HEALING YOUR SUBJUGATION SCHEMA

Enhance Self-Awareness

Maintain a record of instances when you consciously suppress your desires and feelings to accommodate others. This practice will shed light on the patterns triggering your schema. Once you've identified these triggers, observe your behaviour and document your reactions in these situations.

Subsequently, delve into your authentic desires. Even though you have habitually concealed or overlooked them, your innate preferences persist. Begin with simple choices – opting for pink or purple for example, beach or forest – and gradually progress to more profound choices. Reflect on what brings you joy and consider actions you would pursue unencumbered by fear. Honesty with yourself is paramount in this introspective journey.

Assert Yourself

Standing up for yourself can be particularly challenging, especially if you were brought up to associate it with fear or guilt. The misconception that assertiveness equates to pushiness or aggression also contributes to this difficulty. In reality, assertiveness is the honest expression of our wants and feelings.

Revisit the list you created detailing instances of suppressing your needs and identify situations where you could have responded differently. Choose the easiest scenario from this list and practice how you would assert yourself. When the situation arises again, implement what you practised. Gradually extend this practice to more diverse and challenging situations. You may discover that other's reactions are not as extreme as anticipated, which gradually diminishes the association between expressing yourself and fear.

If, however, reactions are consistently adverse, consider evaluating the relationships themselves. Your wants, needs and feelings are as valid and significant as anyone else's and maintaining relationships that respect and acknowledge this is crucial for your well-being.

Embrace Your Challenging Emotions

In the past, expressing your feelings, wants and needs might have triggered feelings of guilt or fear which contributed to your reluctance to be assertive in the present. It's essential to acknowledge that emotions aren't facts, and being assertive doesn't automatically make you a target or selfish. Build your tolerance to these difficult emotions. Meditation and mindfulness can help you to sit with these feelings and accept them for what they are.

Redefine Your Self-Perception

If your actions are driven by a desire to conform to what you believe is most acceptable to others, you might inadvertently be denying people the chance to know and connect with the real you. Embrace vulnerability and gradually allow yourself to be seen. While it feels challenging initially, taking small steps in this direction will become more comfortable over time, providing you with the chance to encounter and connect with individuals who appreciate and resonate with your authentic self.

journal

Journal prompts to help with this schema are:

- What does subjugation mean to you and in what areas of your life do you see this pattern?
- How does this schema manifest in your interactions and decisions?
- What are your essential needs in relationships and for yourself?
- How often do you prioritise your needs and how does this impact your well-being?
- How comfortable are you with setting boundaries?
- What fears or guilt do you associate with asserting your own needs?
- What techniques and strategies can you employ to become more assertive? How can you develop these skills?

13. Self-Sacrifice

Those of you with this schema often struggle to decline requests from others, frequently agreeing to help even when your schedule is tight. This tendency can lead to frustration when your efforts go unrecognised or unacknowledged.

The Origin of the Self-Sacrifice Schema

This schema emerges when a child perceives a parental figure as requiring their help. Such caregivers grapple with mental or physical health challenges or face difficulties in managing various responsibilities, such as caring for younger siblings. When these children receive affirmation or rewards for their helpfulness, they develop an association between their self-worth and prioritising others over themselves. This connection can foster an exaggerated perception of others' helplessness, causing the child to feel guilty when prioritising their own needs and worrying about others' coping abilities in their absence.

How Might You Know if You Have a Self-Sacrifice Schema?

Signs of the self-sacrifice schema are:

- Putting the needs and feelings of others before your own because you believe that this is the right thing to do
- Gravitating to peers who are more vulnerable and need help
- Being helpful in practical or supportive ways
- Feeling tired or overwhelmed due to not catering to your own needs
- Seeing it as your responsibility to help others

HEALING YOUR SELF-SACRIFICE SCHEMA

Although different from the subjugation schema, many of the ways to heal are similar.

Enhance Self-Awareness

Initiate the process by creating a list of instances when you tend to prioritise the needs or emotions of others over your own. It's common for individuals with this schema to harbour an exaggerated perception of other's helplessness. Reflect, taking time to understand your thoughts and feelings whilst discovering your authentic needs for fulfilment. Begin with smaller inquiries and gradually progress to more significant questions, such as identifying the non-negotiables in your relationships and determining areas where collaboration and growth are possible.

Express Yourself

In order to lessen the impact of your emotions (e.g., anger and frustration or guilt) find ways to express them. This could be through journalling or talking to people you trust.

journal

Journal prompts to help with this schema are:

- What does self-sacrifice mean to you?
- In what ways have you noticed yourself behaving in self-sacrificing ways?
- What are your core needs?
- How often do you prioritise your needs and how does self-sacrifice affect your well-being?
- How comfortable are you with setting boundaries?
- What self-care strategies can you implement?

14. Approval Seeking/Recognition

Individuals influenced by this schema often adjust their behaviour based on the company they keep, experiencing a diminished sense of worth if praise is not forthcoming. The significance of status and appearance weigh heavily on their self-perception.

The Origin of the Approval Seeking/Recognition Schema

An approval-seeking schema manifests in families where significant emphasis is placed on external factors. Parents might have exerted control over acceptable activities or the child's educational path. Love and attention could have been contingent on the child meeting the parent's expectations or conforming to specific criteria.

How Might You Know if You Have an Approval Seeking/Recognition Schema?

Signs of this schema are:

- Preoccupation with what others think of you
- Making decisions based on what others think
- Feeling judged or like people won't like you
- Changing how you act or speak depending on others
- Not having a strong sense of identity

- Self-esteem is dependent on how others perceive you
- Money and status are very important to you
- Dwelling on what you have said or done to offend others

HEALING YOUR APPROVAL SEEKING/RECOGNITION SCHEMA

Self-Discovery

Cultivate an understanding of moments that trigger your need for approval from others. Create a list identifying situations where external validation holds significant importance, be it in romantic relationships, friendships or the workplace. Explore your own preferences and be mindful of instances when you don't align with them. Initiate smaller steps, gradually progressing to more significant situations where you actively prioritise your own preferences.

Embrace Your Own Company

For individuals accustomed to seeking approval for validation, solo time initially poses a challenge. However, with consistent practice, you'll discover a growing comfort in your own company and realise that external approval isn't a prerequisite for engaging in activities that bring you joy.

Challenge Your Mindset

For those grappling with this schema, external approval is perceived as a measure of your personal worth. It's crucial to sever this link and recognise your intrinsic value, independent of achievements and external validation. Adopt a compassionate self-dialogue, treating yourself with the kindness you would offer a friend. When triggered, practice positive affirmations such as "I am worthy" or "I have value". Shift your focus from seeking approval to considering the next best step based on your own thoughts and priorities.

Cultivate Mindfulness

Embark on the journey of assertiveness, recognising that the fear of disapproval may surface. Understand that thoughts and emotions are not definitive truths, and expressing yourself assertively doesn't guarantee disapproval. Strengthen your resilience to your own emotions through meditation and mindfulness practices to foster the ability to embrace and accept your feelings and thoughts for what they are.

journal

Journal prompts to help you work on this schema are:

- What does seeking approval mean to you?
- In what areas of your life, do you find yourself seeking approval from others?
- How does this schema manifest in your day-to-day life?
- What are your core values?
- How often do you prioritise these values and how does seeking approval affect them?
- How comfortable are you with accepting and valuing yourself without others' validation?
- What practices can you implement to enhance your self-acceptance?

15. Negativity/Pessimism

Those of you grappling with this schema, tend to lean towards the negative aspects of life and minimise the positive elements. This tendency breeds anxiety and worry, fuelled by the anticipation of things going wrong and an enduring expectation that mistakes will yield severe consequences.

The Origin of the Negativity/Pessimism Schema

Children adopt this schema by mirroring the negative attitudes of their parents or encountering hardship and adversity during childhood, fostering a belief that negative occurrences are the norm. The impact of this schema can extend across generations.

My client, Anya, held this schema and the punitiveness schema when she came for therapy. This schema presented itself through her never expecting that anything good would happen, for fear of disappointment for herself or others. She continually expected the worst, believing that failing was unacceptable, yet inevitable. We worked out that these beliefs stemmed from her mother's own negative outlook and continual fear of negative consequences.

How Might You Know if You Have a Negativity/Pessimism Schema?

- You feel like the world doesn't offer good options and that it's best to accept your situation
- You feel like you're being "realistic" about your limitations
- You avoid new challenges to not reveal your flaws
- You feel that it's better to not get your hopes up for fear of disappointment
- You believe that failing is unacceptable and not a part of growing
- You believe that failing leads to rejection

HEALING YOUR NEGATIVITY/PESSIMISM SCHEMA

Challenge Yourself

Enhance your awareness of thought patterns and their impact on emotions and behaviours. Identify recurring negative thoughts and beliefs, pinpointing the specific situations, people or events that trigger them. This proactive approach allows you to anticipate and manage your responses effectively. Actively challenge and question these negative thoughts by evaluating their basis in concrete evidence versus assumptions or irrational fears.

Anya worked to identify her negative beliefs, which at their core, made her feel that she would ultimately disappoint people.

Foster more positive thinking habits by focusing on the favourable aspects of situations and seeking growth opportunities, even amid challenges. Harness the power of positive affirmations to replace negative beliefs. Repetitively affirm positive statements about yourself and your life to gradually shift your mindset.

Anya started using affirmations, such as "I am enough" to boost her self-esteem, or "Today will be a good day" to boost her positivity.

Cultivate Gratitude

Make a habit of regularly reflecting on the things you're grateful for to shift your focus from negative to positive perspectives. Whether it's as simple as appreciating a sunny day or expressing gratitude for small pleasures like chocolate, actively seek out and note down these moments of positivity in your life.

Anya actively wrote down one thing every day that she was grateful for, this led to her recognising positive things in her day.

Surround Yourself with Positivity

Minimise your exposure to negativity by limiting your engagement with negative news, social media and people who bring negativity into your life. Instead, seek out positive influences. Connect with supportive friends and family members who offer encouragement and understanding. Share your challenges and progress with those who uplift and empower you.

journal

Journal prompts to help you to heal this schema are:

- What are negative thoughts or beliefs you've had about yourself, your life or a specific situation?
- How do your negative thoughts affect your emotions? What emotions do they lead too? How intense are they?
- List three things you're grateful for.
- Describe a recent positive experience. What feelings did it evoke?
- Who do you admire that exhibits a positive outlook? What can you learn from them?

16. Emotional Inhibition

Individuals with the emotional inhibition schema prioritise self-control, often refraining from spontaneous, natural, or playful behaviours. They suppress their own emotional expressions and might discourage others from openly displaying intense feelings.

The Origin of the Emotional Inhibition Schema

This schema originates from a childhood environment where emotions were either discouraged or met with punishment, ignorance or ridicule. Growing up in a family characterised by emotional detachment and a lack of strong emotional connections contributes to the development of this schema.

How Might You Know if You Have an Emotional Inhibition Schema?

Signs of this schema are:

- Feeling flat, emotionless or empty
- Feeling that being emotional isn't your thing
- Avoiding situations where others express emotion or where you are invited to express emotion
- Frustrating loved ones by appearing detached or robotic
- Hiding any emotion that does come up for you

- Feeling emotion in non-personal ways

HEALING YOUR EMOTIONAL INHIBITION SCHEMA

Enhancing Self-Awareness

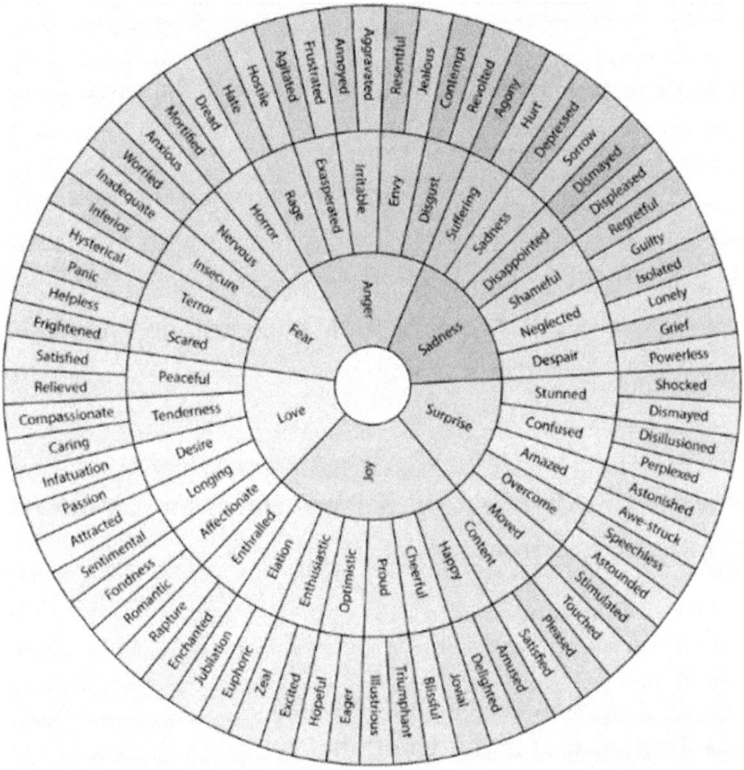

Take time to reflect on occasions when you restrained your emotions and explore the reasons behind this inhibition. Identify patterns in the situations, people or events that tend to trigger emotional inhibition. This will enable you to anticipate and regulate your reactions more effectively. Employ tools like an emotion wheel (See the above image) or journalling to help recognise and label your emotions in the moment. Seek inspiration from individuals who express their emotions openly and learn from their behaviour.

Cultivating Compassion

Extend kindness to yourself and acknowledge that it's completely acceptable to experience a diverse range of emotions without judgement or suppression. Engage in open conversations with friends and family about your emotional journey as sharing these experiences can be therapeutic and validating. For those who find verbal expression challenging, consider exploring creative outlets, such as art, writing or music, as alternative and healthy means of emotional expression. Establish healthy boundaries in your relationships to create a safe space for the authentic and open expression of emotions.

Gradual Emotional Exposure

If specific emotions evoke a strong fear, contemplate the idea of gradual exposure to situations that trigger these emotional responses. Understand that emotions, even uncomfortable ones, are a natural and essential aspect of the human experience, offering valuable insights into your inner world. When emotions become overwhelming, employ techniques such as deep breathing, grounding exercises, or physical activity to facilitate emotional regulation.

journal

Journal prompts to help with this schema are:

- Describe a recent situation in which you felt emotion but had difficulty identifying it? Why do you think it was difficult to identify?
- What fears do you have about expressing your emotions?
- Choose an emotion (e.g., happiness, sadness or anger) and explore it in detail. What does it feel like physically? And emotionally? How do you react when you experience it?
- Write about a recent experience when you wanted to express emotion but held back. What were your reasons for inhibiting the expression?
- Reflect on any recurring patterns of emotional inhibition in your life.
- Who supports you when it comes to your emotions?
- Is there a time when you have fully expressed your emotions? How did it feel?

17. Unrelenting Standards/Hyper-Criticalness

Individuals with this schema often set exceptionally high standards for themselves and others, not necessarily seeking out external validation but driven by an internal desire for personal excellence. This schema is closely linked to perfectionism, an acute attention to detail and a tendency to be highly self-critical.

The Origin of the Unrelenting Standards/Hyper-Criticalness Schema

The development of this schema is often rooted in families where one's worth is closely tied to achievements, with limited emphasis on overall health and well-being. In such environments, criticism outweighs praise, fostering a mindset that perpetually seeks improvement and leaves individuals with the constant feeling that they could achieve even more.

How Might You Know if You Have an Unrelenting Standards/Hyper-Criticalness Schema?

Signs of this schema are:

- Being anxious about your achievements
- Needing to be the best at what you do and giving 100% to everything

- Feeling that whatever you do isn't quite good enough
- Feeling anxious when you aren't using your time productively
- Feelings of guilt when resting
- High standards for yourself and others
- Overly critical of yourself and others

HEALING YOUR UNRELENTING STANDARDS/HYPER-CRITICALNESS SCHEMA

Foster Self-Awareness

Take note of moments when your high standards and self-critical inclinations influence your thoughts and actions. Identify patterns in situations, events or people that trigger your perfectionist tendencies, allowing you to comprehend and navigate your responses more effectively. Actively challenge your perfectionist beliefs. Question whether there is substantial evidence to support them.

Promote Positive Self-Talk

Replace self-criticism with positive and compassionate self-talk. Extend yourself the kindness you would offer a friend. Acknowledge and celebrate small victories and progress, no matter how seemingly insignificant; such positive reinforcement is instrumental in initiating a shift in your mindset. Embrace a new perspective on mistakes, viewing them not as failures but as valuable opportunities for growth and learning.

Evaluate Perfectionism

Contemplate the advantages and drawbacks of perfectionism. Assess its impact on different facets of your life. Begin the process of disentangling your self-worth from your achievements and recognise that your value as a person is not solely contingent on your accomplishments. Acknowledge the inherent impossibility and unsustainability of perfectionism. Cultivate a mindset that embraces imperfection by understanding that flaws and mistakes are inherent aspects of the human experience.

journal

Journal prompts for healing this schema are:

- What are the high standards or expectations you have for yourself?
- Where might these standards have originated? Are they influenced by external factors (Culture, family, society)?
- How has perfectionism contributed to your hyper-criticalness? What are the pros and cons of perfectionism?
- How does hyper-criticalness impact on your emotional well-being?
- Are your standards reasonable? What would be a more balanced standard?
- List your positive qualities and achievements, no matter how small.
- Explore setting more realistic and positive goals. What steps can you take to adjust your expectations?
- What matters to you in life? What are your core values? How do your standards align with them?

18. Punitiveness

The punitiveness schema is defined by a rigid conviction that errors should be met with punishment rather than forgiveness. Individuals with this schema tend to be intolerant and unforgiving, adhering to stringent standards and demonstrating a lack of acceptance for human fallibility, both in themselves and others.

The Origin Of The Punitiveness Schema

The punitiveness schema is frequently shaped by the influence of a caregiver who adopts a highly punitive approach. Children developing this schema often experience critical parenting or caregiving. Growing up with rigid, black and white perspectives on right and wrong contributes to this schema, where the prevailing belief is that mistakes should be met with punishment. This pattern can be generational, passed down from one generation to the next.

My client, Anya, felt that it wasn't acceptable to make mistakes and adopted a critical attitude towards herself. We discovered that growing up, she was never praised when she did well and was instead advised that she could do better. Punishments were often disproportionate and even into adulthood, her parents would overreact to any situation that came up.

How Might You Know if You Have a Punitiveness Schema?

Signs of this schema are:

- An inner voice that expects punishment to improve yourself
- A belief that success only comes through sacrifice and pain
- A feeling that you are behind, or not enough
- A critical tone with yourself and others
- Resenting others for their self-care or rest
- Self-esteem marred by feelings of shame or inadequacy

HEALING YOUR PUNITIVENESS SCHEMA

Enhance Your Self-Esteem

Familiarise yourself with the fundamentals of cultivating healthy self-esteem and establishing robust boundaries. You may have overlooked this aspect in the past due to the influence of your punitiveness schema, which leads you to perceive self-care as selfish. Take note of instances when you employ a punitive tone, both with yourself and with others, and consciously strive to shift towards a more compassionate approach.

Anya started to become more aware when her punitiveness schema was triggered, particularly with her own children and she started to work towards a more compassionate reaction.

Cultivate Self-Compassion

Extend to yourself the same kindness and understanding that you readily provide to a friend; engage in the practice of compassionate self-talk. Additionally, challenge and reframe core beliefs that contribute to your punitive mindset. For instance, if you harbour the belief that mistakes are unacceptable, endeavour to adopt the perspective that mistakes represent opportunities for growth and learning. Embrace forgiveness, not only towards yourself but towards others, as harbouring grudges or resentment can perpetuate punitive thinking and behaviours.

Anya started to work to change her self-critical voice and her views on mistakes, looking instead at what she could learn from them.

Challenge Your Thoughts

Develop an awareness of situations, people or events that trigger punitive thoughts; actively identify and challenge these thoughts as they arise. Assess whether these thoughts are grounded in realistic evidence or if they tend to be overly harsh. Incorporate mindfulness practices to observe your thoughts without judgement. Understand that challenging deeply ingrained beliefs is a gradual process that requires patience. Maintain consistency in practising these new thought patterns.

journal

Journal prompts to help with your punitiveness schema are:

- What does being punitive mean to you?
- Can you identify any specific triggers? How does this schema manifest in your daily life and self - perception?
- What self-critical beliefs do you hold about yourself? How valid are these beliefs?
- How comfortable are you with practicing self-compassion and forgiveness?
- What would it feel like to respond to your mistakes with compassion?
- What techniques or practices can you employ to enhance self-compassion?

It is important to note that your schemas will play into your attachment type and vice versa, continually impacting how you approach interactions with others.

As we conclude this chapter, take a moment to contemplate how your schemas impact you and how you can work towards minimalizing this impact.

- What have you learned?
- How are you going to implement this?

Chapter 5

Generational Issues Within Families

In the past century, family dynamics and structures have undergone profound transformations. The conventional model of mothers staying at home while fathers worked has evolved, giving way to a diverse range of family compositions. Nuclear families are no longer the predominant structure, as society witnesses the rise of single-parent households, same-sex parenting, children being raised by grandparents or other family members, blended families, polyamorous families and various other configurations. It is important to talk about generational issues as they will have a profound impact on your upbringing and worldview.

This evolving landscape reflects a departure from traditional norms. The concept of the generation gap encapsulates differences in opinions, values, attitudes and behaviours between distinct age groups, often manifested in parent-child relationships or between older and younger individuals. Negotiating these generational disparities can lead to misunderstandings and conflicts within families.

Generational issues include:

Parental Respect Across Generations

The approach to parenting has evolved over the years, with younger parents tending to emphasise equality in their relationships with children, a departure from the mindset of older generations. Today's grandparents and great-grandparents often grew up with the notion that children should be seen and not heard, emphasising the importance of demonstrating respect for elders, even in situations where it is not warranted. In contrast to earlier generations, where obedience and parental discipline were paramount, today's children are encouraged to question and express themselves. However, this shift in parenting styles can result in challenges, as older individuals view contemporary parenting as lenient or lacking in respect. If raised with the belief that questioning authority is discouraged, individuals will struggle with curiosity and face difficulties expressing emotions openly.

Personal experiences with parenting approaches can create tensions in relationships, as seen in my own marriage. My wife, who is ten years older than me, was raised in a more traditional setting and finds our children questioning her authority when it's intended to keep them safe, a challenge. I have a more permissive parenting approach and encourage their curiosity. She was raised to not excessively display emotion and can find their emotional outbursts frustrating. These generational differences in parenting styles highlight the ongoing evolution of family dynamics.

Bridging the Technology Gap

In the past century, technology has undergone unprecedented transformations, revolutionising the way we communicate. Older generations, accustomed to writing handwritten letters, will not have encountered computers until later in life. In contrast, today's children are exposed to technology from birth, and seamlessly integrate it into their daily lives, using computers as educational tools. This difference in experience becomes evident in social settings, where older family members find activities like texting at the dinner table to be impolite and grapple with the nuances of the evolving social networking phenomenon.

The intrusion of social media into personal lives has sparked concerns among older generations, who value privacy differently than their younger counterparts. This technology gap underscores the shifting dynamics in communication and highlights the need for understanding and adapting to the rapid changes brought about by technological advancements.

Technology plays a pivotal role in shaping the way we communicate, form romantic connections and engage in leisure activities. It has created noticeable gaps between generations. For instance, my wife, not having grown up with texting as a primary means of communication, tends to be less inclined to check her phone promptly, occasionally leaving me waiting for urgent replies.

The current pace of our lives is marked by immediacy; a stark contrast to my childhood, when waiting days for the next episode of a favourite TV show was the norm. Now, binge-watching an entire series within a couple of days is the new standard. While technology grants children newfound independence, it also fosters impatience, as the instant access they enjoy diminishes the need for waiting, a phenomenon that was absent in the past. This evolving technological landscape continues to redefine the dynamics of communication and lifestyle.

This disparity in technological experience can lead to communication and understanding challenges among family members. For instance, my mother, who was born in the 1940s and is older than a lot of my friend's parents, struggled to comprehend the fear of missing out I felt as the only child in my class without Sky TV. This technology gap extends to present-day parenting, introducing concerns related to screen time, online safety and ensuring access to appropriate content. Balancing these generational differences in technology usage poses distinct challenges, shaping the dynamics of family life in the contemporary age.

Transformations in Work Ethics and Educational Goals

The landscape of work and education has undergone remarkable shifts in the last century. In contemporary times, it's common for individuals to change careers multiple times, and many opt for a continual pursuit of education, adopting the roles of permanent students. In contrast, older generations often faced constraints on educational opportunities and juggled multiple jobs to support their families. Financial priorities were directed towards savings, and indulgences were limited. However, the present-day ethos tends to emphasise immediate gratification, with a focus on spending, rather than saving for retirement. Work is often seen as a means to fulfil personal desires.

Personal experiences from older generations, like my mother, who was encouraged to leave school at fifteen and start working, reflect a different era, where education was a luxury. This historical perspective can manifest in pushy attitudes towards achievement, as seen in my own upbringing, which contributes to the development of a failure schema, as discussed in the preceding chapter.

An additional impact for me stems from my mother's background, rooted in a generation where women shouldered the responsibilities of both homemaking and full-time employment. In instances where I delegate housework tasks to my wife, my mother often perceives it as laziness, reflecting the expectations ingrained in her era. Navigating this perspective has been crucial for me, learning not to internalise these views, but instead challenging them and recognising the evolving dynamics of gender roles and responsibilities.

Embracing Autonomy

Modern values emphasise the importance of individuals expressing themselves and asserting their independence from an early age. Young children today confidently voice their opinions to authority figures, a behaviour less common in older generations who believed in allowing kids to remain carefree for as long as possible. These differing perspectives on autonomy can generate tension within families. For instance, my own mother, belonging to an older generation, adopted a more protective parenting style compared to my peers' parents. This approach, whilst rooted in care, inadvertently fuelled my fear of missing out, prompting me to engage in behaviours such as becoming less trustworthy and sneaking around. The evolving dynamics of autonomy and parenting styles contribute to the complex interplay of generational differences within families.

As we conclude this chapter, take a moment to contemplate how the generational gap has affected you.

- What have you learned?
- How will you implement it?

Chapter 6

Healing the Generational Gap

Initiating the process of bridging the generational gap involves actively listening to the perspectives of each family member. In my case, I took the step of asking my Mum about her push for education, and she shared that it stemmed from her own lack of support in pursuing education and the sincere desire for me to have a different experience. This insight greatly enhanced my understanding of her motivations.

The key is to foster open communication and encourage family members to talk and listen without judgement. Creating a space where opinions can be expressed freely allows both older and younger individuals to share their thoughts, feelings and perspectives, paving the way for mutual understanding and connection. If communication with the family members is not possible, work towards understanding and forgiveness.

Strive to nurture a culture of respect within the family to ensure that the values, opinions and experiences of each generation are not only heard but genuinely understood. Foster an environment that promotes the exchange of knowledge and life experiences between different age groups. Younger individuals stand to gain valuable insights and wisdom from the wealth of experiences of their older counterparts. Simultaneously, older generations can benefit from the fresh perspectives and innovative ideas brought forth by the younger members of the family. In this way, a dynamic intergenerational exchange can flourish which enriches the family culture and fosters mutual appreciation.

Take a moment to recognise and embrace the diversity that exists both within and between generations in your family. Each generation brings a unique set of experiences and perspectives, contributing to the rich and intricate tapestry that defines your family. By acknowledging and appreciating these differences, you lay the foundation for a more inclusive and understanding family structure. Celebrating the varied qualities of each generation fosters an environment where every family member feels valued, ultimately strengthening the bonds that weave through your family's shared history.

journal

Journal prompts to help you explore this are:

- How would you describe your relationship with your parents or older family members during your childhood? What are specific memories that stand out?
- What generational differences or conflicts did you experienced growing up? How did these affect your relationships?
- What values, traditions or beliefs have been passed down to you? How do you feel about these values? Do you wish to carry them forwards?
- How do you view the world differently to older family members? What are the reasons for these differences?
- What positive qualities or wisdom have you gained from older generations?
- What are your hopes and aspirations for future generations in your family?

As we conclude this chapter, take a moment to contemplate how the generational gap has affected you and how you can work towards minimalizing this impact.

- What have you learned?
- How will you implement it?

Chapter 7

Love Languages

The concept of love languages, introduced by Dr Gary Chapman in his 1992 book, "The Five Love Languages," revolves around the idea that individuals express and perceive love in distinct ways. Gaining insight into these love languages can significantly enhance the quality of relationships, whether romantic or with family and friends. It's important to address our Love Language as it develops through our childhood experience it is crucial to understand how you give and receive love as you undertake your healing journey.

Often, we instinctively give love in the manner we prefer to receive it, leading to potential miscommunications. For instance, my wife's love language is acts of service; she feels most loved when I assist with household chores or prepare a meal. While she reciprocates these actions, my primary love language is Words of Affirmation – I feel cherished through compliments, words of encouragement and support. Consequently, when she cooks for me, or I express how amazing she is, the intended love may not be received in the way it is intended. Understanding and aligning with each other's love language can profoundly enrich the fabric of relationships.

The Five Love Languages

There are five distinct ways through which individuals express and receive love:

- **Words of Affirmation –** You cherish verbal expressions of love and appreciation. Compliments, words of encouragement and affectionate expressions hold paramount significance for you.
- **Acts of Service –** For you, actions carry more weight than words. Feeling loved occurs when someone takes tangible steps to assist with tasks or chores.
- **Receiving gifts –** You find value in receiving thoughtful gifts as symbols of love and consideration. These need not be extravagant but should reflect thoughtfulness and effort.
- **Quality Time -** You place importance on spending meaningful, undivided attention with your loved ones. Feeling loved involves being the sole focus without distractions.
- **Physical Touch -** You feel loved through physical affection, such as hugs, kisses, hand-holding or cuddling.

Understanding and appreciating these diverse love languages can significantly deepen connections and contribute to more fulfilling relationships.

How This is Impacted by Your Family

Love languages take shape and evolve during childhood under the influence of various factors, including the family environment, experiences with caregivers and early relationships. Key influences include:

Observing and Absorbing

As children, we are remarkably observant and susceptible to influence, closely observing the interactions and expressions of love within our families from parents and caregivers. These early observations wield substantial influence in shaping our understanding of love and its proper modes of expression. In my own upbringing, my mum consistently imparted words of affirmation, showering me with verbal expressions of love. It follows logically that as an adult, I find a need for such affirmations to feel loved.

Parent-Child Interactions

The dynamics of interaction with our parents or primary caregivers wield a substantial impact on the development of our love languages. For instance, if you received abundant cuddles and kisses during childhood, there's a higher likelihood of developing physical touch as a primary love language As an illustration, my wife, whose family weren't overly affectionate, places more significance on acts of service or quality time as expressions of love.

Behavioural Reinforcement in Childhood

Children often adopt specific behaviours based on the responses they receive from their parents. For instance, if a child consistently receives praise of positive feedback for contributing to household chores, they will develop an acts of service love language.

Influence of the Emotional Environment

The emotional atmosphere within a home plays a crucial role in shaping a child's development of love languages. A household characterised by consistent verbal affirmation and encouragement, for example, is likely to nurture words of affirmation as a prominent love language.

As we conclude this chapter, take a moment to contemplate how your Love Language impacts you.

- What have you learned?
- How are you going to implement this?

Chapter 8

Adapting and Expanding Your Ability to Express and Receive Love

To embark on the journey of adapting and broadening your ability to give and receive love, the initial step is gaining awareness of your current love language. Numerous quizzes are available online for this purpose, or you can reflect on past relationships to work out which love language resonates with you the most.

Moving forward, effective communication with your partner and those around you is crucial. Express your own love language and ask about theirs. Achieving an understanding of how individuals both give and receive love is fundamental to meeting each other's emotional needs.

Although your primary love language is deeply ingrained, remain open to the possibility that it can evolve over time. Personal experiences, individual growth and the dynamics of your relationships can shape how you both give and receive love. Experiment with expressing love in various ways by adapting to the love languages of your partner or family. For instance, if your partner's love language is acts of service, engage in thoughtful gestures or acts of kindness. This exploration may unveil a newfound enjoyment in expressing love beyond your primary love language.

Embarking on a journey of self-improvement and personal development is key to becoming a more well-rounded individual. This, in turn, enhances your adaptability and openness to different love languages. As you delve into understanding the love language of others, your empathy grows. Consistently practice empathy by stepping into the shoes of those around you, seeking to comprehend their needs and desires. Be willing to make an effort to meet these needs, even if they diverge from your own primary love language.

Whilst you will have a primary love language, you will also have secondary love languages. Incorporating aspects of these into your relationships will make them more fulfilling and allow you to recognise and receive love more effectively.

Love languages are not rigid and can evolve over time. The key is to be open, communicative and willing to adapt to the needs of others, whilst expressing your love in a way that feels genuine to you, with your ultimate goal being to create loving and fulfilling relationships with those around you.

journal

- What is your current love language and how has it influenced your past relationships and interactions with loved ones?
- Have you noticed any change or conflicts in your relationships that might be related to differences in love languages?
- Are there any instances in the past where you have felt unloved or misunderstood? How did your love language contribute?
- What goals or improvements do you hope to achieve by adapting your love language?
- How do the love language of your partner, family and friends differ from yours and how has this impacted your relationships?
- How can a better understanding of another's love language enhance your ability to connect with them?
- How did your family upbringing impact on your love language and perception of love?
- What steps can you take to become more proficient in expressing love?
- How can improving your understanding of your own love language contribute to more fulfilling and balanced relationships?

As we conclude this chapter, take a moment to contemplate how love languages impact you and how you can work towards altering this impact.

- What have you learned?
- How will you implement it?

Chapter 9

Inner Child

The concept of the inner child revolves around the psychological and emotional idea that within every adult, certain aspects retain the thoughts, feelings and vulnerabilities carried from childhood – these aspects are our inner children. The inner child embodies the early experiences and emotions that have played a pivotal role in shaping an individual's identity, beliefs and behaviours. It serves as a symbolic representation of one's younger self. Frequently employed in therapy, the inner child concept becomes a tool for comprehending and addressing past emotional wounds and unresolved issues, aiming at fostering understanding and healing. Exploring your inner child is vital, as reparenting and healing these parts of you will be a crucial part of cycle-breaking and healing.

What is Your Inner Child?

Emotional Wounds

The concept of the inner child is closely tied to past emotional wounds or traumas, encompassing childhood experiences or significant events that left a lasting impact on your emotional well-being.

Unmet Needs

Your inner child may symbolise unmet emotional needs from your childhood years, including the longing for love, validation, security or attention. The lingering effects of unfulfilled needs can persist, shaping emotions and behaviours well into adulthood.

Let's come back to my client, Maisie, who previously sought love and acceptance through various external and detrimental avenues. Her endeavours involved a fixation on appearance and job titles. She adopted a chameleon-like approach, shaping herself according to others' expectations or societal norms. Unfortunately, these efforts were often directed towards individuals incapable of providing the desired acceptance, including bosses at work, romantic partners and transient connections. Through the therapeutic process, we unravelled that Maisie's actions were fuelled by an unmet need for unconditional love and acceptance during her childhood. This revelation illuminated how her inner child was still fervently reaching for these essential emotional pillars.

Inner Dialogue

Your inner child plays a significant role in influencing your inner dialogue and self-talk. Negative thought patterns and self-criticism often trace back to early experiences and messages absorbed during childhood, highlighting the enduring impact of childhood on your emotional landscape.

Recognising Your Inner Child

The process of identifying your inner child stands as a crucial milestone in fostering self-awareness and beginning emotional healing. It's essential to acknowledge that connecting with your inner child is a deeply personal and emotional experience that requires both time and self-compassion. As you explore and comprehend how your past has shaped your present, the ultimate objective is to cultivate a profound understanding of yourself, mend emotional wounds, and nurture the vulnerable yet authentic facets of your inner child. Various approaches can aid in recognising and establishing a connection with your inner child, including:

Reflecting on Your Childhood

Take time to reflect and delve into the reservoir of your childhood memories, experiences and relationships with family and caregivers. Reflect on significant events and the array of emotions that accompanied them. Utilise tools such as childhood photos or keepsakes to establish a connection with your younger self, recognising that visual cues possess the potential to trigger memories and evoke emotions intricately linked with your inner child.

Journalling

Building on earlier discussions, engaging in journal writing serves as a valuable tool for delving into the intricacies of your emotions and thoughts linked to your childhood. Take the opportunity to articulate your early experiences, delve into the dynamics of past relationships and shine a light on any lingering unresolved issues or emotional wounds that have transcended into your adulthood. Journalling provides a safe space to unravel the layers of your past, fostering self-awareness and contributing to your ongoing journey of healing and self-discovery.

Emotional Triggers

Be mindful of situations or experiences that evoke strong emotional reactions within you. These emotional triggers frequently trace their roots back to childhood experiences, offering valuable insights into the needs and wounds of your inner child. Attuning to these triggers provides a lens through which you can better understand and address the deeper layers of your emotional landscape.

Guided Meditation and Visualisation

You can use guided meditation or visualisation techniques to connect with your inner child, in these exercises you can imagine meeting with and nurturing your younger self, providing the love and care that you needed as a child.

When undertaking a visualisation exercise, find a quiet and comfortable place to sit or lie down, close your eyes and take a few deep and relaxing breaths.

Visualisations you can try are:

- **The safe place visualisation:** Imagine a safe and peaceful place from your childhood, such as a favourite park, a childhood home or a place where you felt loved and secure. Visualise yourself as a child in that safe place, playing or simply being happy. Engage with your inner child in the safe environment, talk to them and ask them how they are feeling. Provide comfort, assurance and love to your inner child and offer them any support or protection they need.
- **The mirror visualisation:** Sit in front of a mirror in a quiet room. Gaze into your own eyes in the reflection and imagine the reflection transforming into your younger self, around the age you feel your inner child is. Visualise this younger self looking at you with curiosity, trust or vulnerability. Speak to your younger self in your mind; ask how they feel and what they need.

- **The inner child's room visualisation:** Imagine walking down a corridor and arriving at a door that represents your inner child's room. Open the door and enter the room. Visualise the surroundings, the colours and the objects that represent your inner child's world. Look for your inner child who will be drawing, playing or doing something they enjoy. Approach your inner child and engage in a loving and nurturing conversation.
- **Letter writing visualisation:** Sit in a quiet space with a pen and paper. Imagine yourself as a child and write a letter from your inner child to your present self. Allow your inner child to express their feelings, needs and desires in the letter. After writing the letter, respond to it as your present self, offering love, support and understanding.

Inner child exercises

Engage in inner child work exercises, which involve activities such as drawing, colouring or writing letters to your inner child. This can help you to express and process your emotions.

Examples of inner child activities are:

- **Art and creativity:** Colouring or creating your own drawings and paintings, crafting, including activities like making friendship bracelets, collages or origami, building with Lego or other construction sets, writing stories, poetry or Journalling to express your thoughts and feelings.

- **Play and Imagination:** Play with toys or action figures from your childhood, create and play with a dollhouse or miniature world, engage in imaginative play such as pretending to be a superhero, princess or explorer, build forts or play in a playhouse, treehouse or tent.
- **Outdoor play:** Swing on a swing set or go down a slide at a playground, play outdoor games like tag, hide-and-seek or hopscotch, blow bubbles, fly a kite or have a picnic in a park. Ride a bike or skateboard.
- **Games and puzzles:** Play board games, card games or video games that you enjoyed as a child. Solve puzzles such as jigsaws or crosswords or engage in physical games such as tag, football or skipping.
- **Music and dance:** Listen to music from your childhood or songs that make you feel joyful, dance freely around the room, expressing yourself through movement or play musical instruments such as the piano, guitar or drums.
- **Nurturing activities:** Cuddle with a stuffed animal or favourite blanket, practice self-care activities like taking a bubble bath, getting a massage or enjoying a spa day, curl up with a good book or read children's stories.

- **Nature Exploration:** Take a nature walk or hike and explore the outdoors, collect rocks, leaves or flowers, have a nature scavenger hunt or go on a treasure hunt in your garden or a nearby park.
- **Food and treats:** Bake and decorate biscuits, cupcakes or your favourite childhood treats, make a blanket fort and have a picnic inside with your favourite snacks, try comfort foods that remind you of your childhood.
- **Self-expression:** Dress up in costumes or outfits that make you feel happy and playful. Express your emotions through art, dance or music. Keep a dream journal to explore your inner world.
- **Letters to your inner child:** Write letters to your inner child, offering love, support and encouragement. Create a journal where you and your inner child can communicate back and forth, share feelings and track progress in your healing journey.

Observe your inner dialogue

Be attentive to your self-dialogue and the beliefs you harbour about yourself. Observe closely for any reoccurring patterns of self-criticism or self-doubt that might be linked to the unmet needs or past emotional wounds of your inner child. Recognising these patterns provides an opportunity to nurture self-awareness and explore avenues for healing and self-compassion.

As we conclude this chapter, take a moment to contemplate how your inner child impacts you.

- What have you learned?
- How are you going to implement this?

Chapter 10

Healing Your Inner Child

Having gained insights into identifying and connecting with your inner child, let's look further into the transformative journey of healing your inner child wounds. This process entails nurturing, understanding and addressing emotional wounds from your past. It involves a conscious acknowledgement and embrace of the vulnerable, yet authentic facets of your younger self, fostering a compassionate approach to your own emotional well-being.

Self-Awareness

Initiate the process by reflecting on your past and childhood experiences. Identify any lingering emotional wounds, traumas or unresolved issues that might be exerting an influence on your adult life. Whilst it will initially feel strange to envision opening up to your younger self, consider inner child work as a journey of self-discovery. A vital aspect of this self-discovery involves recognising and accepting the elements that caused you pain in childhood. Bringing these hurts to the forefront of your consciousness is a crucial step towards understanding their enduring impact.

Dedicate time to reflection, focussing on your past and childhood experiences. Journalling about your memories, feelings and emotions can be instrumental in gaining profound insights. Delve into your emotional reactions and triggers, taking note of situations or events that elicit strong emotional responses, as they are intricately linked to unresolved issues within your inner child. Additionally, be attuned to reoccurring patterns in your adult life, particularly those intertwined with relationships, behaviours, and beliefs. Recognise that these patterns trace back to your childhood experiences. Set aside regular time for self-reflection and check-ins with your inner child. Ask yourself how your inner child is feeling, what they need and how you can support them.

journal

Visualise and connect with your inner child, using the visualisation exercises already mentioned, to establish the relationship with this part of yourself. Journal about your inner child and investigate their feelings, needs and experiences.

Journal prompts that might help with this are:

- What are your earliest childhood memories, how do they make you feel?
- Describe your favourite childhood games or activities? How did they bring you joy?
- Reflect on your relationships when you were a child. What positive and negative emotions do these memories evoke?
- Write a letter to your younger self, offering love, support and encouragement. What advice would you give to your inner child?
- How have your inner child's needs (both met and unmet) shaped your adult self and your current relationships?
- Explore any painful experiences from your childhood. How have these impacted in adulthood?
- What would you have liked to experience or receive as a child?
- Reflect on moments you felt most secure or loved as a child. What circumstances or relationships contributed to these feelings?
- Write about the dreams, aspirations or talents you had as a child. Have you pursued them or have they been neglected over time?

Cultivating Self-Compassion

Starting to connect with your inner child can be an intense and transformative experience. During this process, extend to yourself the same kindness, understanding and nurturing care that you would offer to a cherished friend. Recognise that your inner child is deserving of love, support and validation. To achieve this, practice acknowledging the emotions of your inner child without judgement and grant yourself permission to feel and express these emotions in a healthy manner.

Validate your inner child's experiences and feelings, affirming that they are not only heard but are valued. Prioritise self-care practices that promote emotional well-being, such as meditation, mindfulness, yoga and relaxation techniques.

As we conclude this chapter, take a moment to contemplate how your inner child impacts you and how you can start to heal.

- What have you learned?
- How are you going to implement this?

Chapter 11

Reparenting Your Inner Child

Reparenting your inner child is akin to assuming the role of caregiver to an actual child - you offer support and become a secure attachment figure, but this time, for yourself. Provide your inner child with the essential elements for their well-being - safety, support, tenderness and kindness. By embracing this process, you empower your inner child to not only survive but also flourish. As you engage in the reparenting journey, you find that your skills, kindness and compassion grow, aligning with the resolution of your own personal issues.

Reparenting involves a number of steps:

1. Rediscovering your inner child

Building on our earlier discussion about identifying and connecting with your inner child, let's explore a practical approach. Delving into key memories that have left a lasting impact can provide insights into the age you were and the experiences that have shaped you. Through meditation, observe your thoughts from the perspective of your inner child, attuning to their tone, whether sad, relaxed, irritated or afraid. Familiarise yourself with these inner voices. Examining childhood photos can offer a visual exploration of how that younger version of you experienced the world.

2. Establishing connection with your inner child

Now that you've acknowledged the presence of your inner child, the next step is to ensure they know you're there for them. Assume the role of a kind, caring and present adult parent who adapts to meet the child where they are. Initiate contact by introducing yourself and observing their response, employing visualisation or journalling between yourself and your inner child. Cultivate rapport, trust and a profound sense of connection. Enquire with your inner child about their needs and make a dedicated effort to fulfil those needs in healthy and constructive ways.

3. Enhance Communication

Once the connection with your inner child is established, active listening becomes paramount. Pay close attention to the emotions that arise in response to situations triggering strong reactions or discomfort, unearthing old wounds like anger from unmet needs, feelings of abandonment or rejection, insecurity, vulnerability, guilt, shame or anxiety. Cultivate a receptive mindset and embrace these feelings with attentive acknowledgement and validation. This approach forges an environment of understanding and paves the way for effective communication and healing.

Allocate dedicated moments for self-reflection and attentively examine the tone of your internal dialogue. Take note of whether it leans towards negativity or self-affirmation. Intentionally steer your thoughts towards positivity by incorporating affirmations tailored to address specific challenges you encounter. Embrace the habit of articulating love and appreciation for yourself, even if it feels unfamiliar initially. Acknowledge that you are your most formidable ally, actively cultivating a supportive and affirming relationship with yourself.

Be attentive to the tone of your inner dialogue - does it echo the voices of your parents, an authoritative teacher or a sibling? Additionally, observe the qualities you extend to your inner child - do you embody patience, kindness, acceptance or firmness? Acknowledge that as adults, embodying qualities we didn't receive in childhood can be challenging. However, as you engage in the healing process for your inner child, you will discover these qualities gradually become more accessible and natural for you to embody.

4. Build Trust

The various facets of our inner children often serve as protective mechanisms, coping strategies, or defences developed to shield us from challenging experiences. Consider these mechanisms as self-protective measures, rooted in a genuine desire for self-care. For instance, in my case, due to the high academic expectations set out by my mum during my childhood, my inner child tends to procrastinate – a defence mechanism preventing potential disappointment if I fall short of these expectations. Whilst self-protection is an act of self-love, it can transform into self-sabotage when no longer suitable, as exemplified by my procrastination habits. Recognising and understanding these protective strategies is essential for fostering trust within yourself and dismantling patterns that hinder personal growth. For me, procrastination has held me back for many years, but now that I understand this pattern, I am able to overcome it.

Establishing communication with the self-sabotaging aspects of ourselves becomes more effective when rooted in a shared understanding of the love and care that underlie these protective measures. By recognising and acknowledging the positive intention behind these behaviours, our communication with these aspects becomes more harmonious, paving the way for smoother healing and transformation.

Demonstrating to your inner child parts what trust looks and feels like is a pivotal step in fostering a sense of security. As you exemplify trustworthiness, these inner child parts gradually learn to trust you, laying the foundation for the development of healthy relationships with those aspects of yourself. This, in turn, allows you to collaboratively engage with these inner child parts, guiding them towards the acquisition of constructive skills instead of perpetuating sabotaging patterns. For me, a vital part of my process was communicating with my inner child, that it was ok to fail and get it wrong.

5. Find out what they need

Discovering and acknowledging our pain, tending to its wounds, and allowing it to gracefully pass are essential steps in our self-healing journey. To address the persistent pain that we've clung to, it becomes crucial to revisit and connect with our past selves.

Certain aspects of our inner child are unfamiliar with their needs, having never experienced or labelled them. For instance, some inner children lack the comprehension of essential emotional elements like validation. Recognising that validation is often a fundamental requirement for these inner aspects can pave the way for understanding and meeting their unmet needs.

6. Provide what they need

Your inner child yearns for emotional support, playfulness, cuddles or love. Regardless of their presentation, age or specific needs, your inner child requires your consistent presence and engagement.

Whether it involves embracing play, demonstrating self-care and love, providing validation, or penning a heartfelt letter to yourself, it's essential to heed your instincts and respond to what these inner aspects crave. Be attuned to their needs. Offer the nurturing and attention that fosters a compassionate connection with yourself.

You will find yourself lacking certain life skills that weren't imparted by your parents, necessitating self-guided learning in adulthood. Reparenting yourself involves addressing these gaps whether they pertain to decision-making, navigating uncomfortable emotions, honing communication, establishing boundaries, or even cultivating the capacity to love. Recognising and actively engaging in the process of acquiring these skills becomes a vital aspect of your personal growth and self-nurturing journey.

Inner Dialogue

Regularly observe and fine-tune your inner dialogue, consciously substituting negative self-talk and self-criticism with compassionate and uplifting affirmations. Challenge and reframe beliefs that no longer positively contribute to your growth, especially those rooted in childhood experiences. Utilise positive affirmations as a transformative tool. As an example, when encountering negative thoughts, such as "If you don't try your best, it won't matter if you fail" which is a classic one of my own, replace it with the affirming statement "Success means trying your best" the intentional shift in perspective has been instrumental in altering my mindset, alleviating the fear of failure, and addressing anxieties held by my inner child.

Emotional Release

Grant yourself the space to acknowledge and liberate any lingering emotions tied to past wounds. Explore diverse outlets for catharsis, including traditional methods like crying and talking, as well as engaging in emotional release techniques such as:

- Journalling
- Artistic expression
- Deep breathing
- Physical activity
- Vocal release through screaming or shouting
- Mindfulness or meditation
- Progressive muscle relaxation
- Body movement
- The uplifting power of laughter

Embracing a multifaceted approach allows you to tailor your emotional release to your individual needs, fostering a holistic and healing experience.

Forgiveness

Forgiveness doesn't mean condoning or excusing hurtful behaviours, it's a process of releasing the anger and resentment you carry. Endeavour to forgive individuals, such as parents or caregivers, who have played a role in your past wounds. In the upcoming chapters, we'll delve into developing a deeper understanding of them. Strive to view the situation from alternating perspectives; comprehending motivations and circumstances can pave the way for a more manageable path to forgiveness.

Forgiveness constitutes a pivotal stride in the journey of healing. Equally crucial is extending forgiveness to yourself and releasing any self-blame, guilt or shame lingering from past experiences. It's vital to recognise and validate your emotions; it's permissible to feel hurt, angry or betrayed. Allow yourself to fully experience these emotions as part of your healing process.

To facilitate this process, consider composing a forgiveness letter - an expressive outlet designed, not necessarily for sending, but for articulating your emotions, extending forgiveness and liberating yourself from negative sentiments.

Setting Boundaries

Creating and maintaining healthy boundaries is crucial for safeguarding your inner child from potential harm. Asserting the power to say no, free from guilt, when required, plays a pivotal role in cultivating a secure and supportive environment conducive to the flourishing of your inner child.

Initiating the establishment of boundaries begins with acknowledging your personal limits and comfort zones. Reflect on various aspects, including relationships, work dynamics, friendships and self-care practices. Recognise that boundaries serve as a fundamental aspect of self-care, acting as a shield for your emotional well-being. They play a crucial role in safeguarding you from exposure to potentially harmful or triggering situations and emphasise the importance of prioritising your mental and emotional health.

Establish boundaries with others through clear and respectful communication of your needs and limits. This involves articulating your feelings, confidently saying no when necessary and seeking support when needed. A crucial aspect of maintaining emotional safety is identifying and distancing yourself from toxic or harmful relationships that pose a threat to your inner child. Prioritising this boundary is paramount for safeguarding your emotional well-being.

Consistency plays a crucial role; persistently strengthen and refine your boundaries as you gain insights into what brings a sense of safety and support for you. Establishing and upholding healthy boundaries throughout your inner child healing journey serves as a protective and nurturing measure. This practice enables the cultivation of a loving, secure environment conducive to the healing and growth of your inner child – by prioritising emotional well-being and self-compassion, it becomes an indispensable component of the overall healing process.

As we conclude this chapter, take a moment to contemplate how you can reparent your inner child.

- What have you learned?
- How will you implement it?

Chapter 12

Embracing Your Shadow Self

What is Your Shadow Self?

Your shadow self encompasses the facets of your identity that you tend to reject – the darker corners that harbour repressed instincts, ideas and negative emotions. Many of us instinctively conceal these aspects, especially those bearing the uncomfortable feelings of hurt, guilt, shame, ridicule, loneliness, anger or sadness. It's not uncommon for me to hear my clients disassociate from certain traits, asserting statements like "I'm not an angry person" or "I don't let myself feel sad", distancing themselves from less favourable aspects. Coined by Carl Jung, the concept of a shadow self invites exploration into these hidden dimensions of your psyche. It's important to explore our shadow as, in order to heal, we need to integrate our shadow parts.

Consider this scenario: as a child, you faced ridicule for being exceptionally quiet. This led to internal questioning about potential flaws, prompting you to override your natural inclination and force yourself to be more vocal, even against your own needs. Fast forward, years later, someone innocuously comments, "You're a bit quiet today" and it deeply unsettles you. Although the comment carries no ill intent, you emotionally connect with it as an affront, due to the historical label, and childhood ridicule. This seemingly harmless observation about your quietness now feels like an attack on your entire identity. Consequently, the notion of being quiet is rejected in your subconscious, gradually morphing into an integral part of your shadow self. These disregarded fragments often stem from adverse childhood experiences.

Neglecting Your Shadow Self

Disregarding your shadow self can detrimentally affect your self-perception and distort your understanding of truth and reality. The aspects relegated to your shadow have likely been dismissed or even ridiculed, akin to your inner child yearning for understanding and exploration. It's entirely feasible to embrace these shadows without letting them dictate your behaviour.

For example, upon recognising a manipulative tendency within my own shadow self, I've learned to navigate and control it. Acknowledging these aspects empowers me to maintain a healthier sense of self-awareness and control.

Despite efforts to evade your shadow, it remains an intrinsic part of you, inevitably surfacing as a trigger, bringing forth repressed emotions. This manifestation can lead to challenges such as diminished self-esteem, a tendency to judge others, losing sight of your inherent talents, and potential mental health issues. The discomfort arising from confronting your shadow drives you to project judgements onto others who exhibit similar traits. Acknowledging and addressing these shadow aspects is crucial for fostering personal growth and maintaining mental well-being.

Engaging in Shadow Work

Engaging in shadow work is a vital component of your healing journey. Until we successfully integrate our shadow parts, they persist in making themselves known, whether we actively acknowledge them or not. Striving to become the best version of ourselves necessitates viewing our entirety, embracing the complete picture, encompassing both light and dark aspects. Key benefits to shadow work include:

- **Emotional Healing** - Confronting and embracing suppressed emotions, traumas and fears within the shadow can pave the way for emotional healing. Acknowledging these emotions can contribute to greater emotional well-being. Working on your shadow allows you to foster a journey towards authenticity and a more genuine self.
- **Boost Self-confidence -** Embracing the entirety of yourself leads to increased control and

confidence. Letting go of shame or dislike fosters a greater comfort within, making you better equipped to manage and minimise any uncomfortable characteristics. Self-awareness allows for active work on these aspects; for instance, recognising manipulative tendencies enables conscious prevention. Confronting and embracing challenging facets cultivates resilience, empowering you to navigate difficulties with heightened self-assurance and adaptability.

- **Embrace Creativity** – Your shadow doesn't only conceal undesirable traits; it can hide wonderful aspects of yourself, such as creativity. Accepting your shadow side enables you to uncover and embrace these positive aspects. Let's look at Jessica, a client of mine, who despite having a deep passion for art as a child, had suppressed her talents due to parental discouragement. Her parents valued academia over creativity. Through shadow work in therapy, we unveiled her artistic abilities and Jessica even began to use them as a means to express emotions, showcasing the transformative power of acknowledging and nurturing the creative facets within
- **Enhance your interactions** – Embracing your entire self is the key to extending the same acceptance to others. By seeing and accepting people as they are, rather than as reflections of aspects you dislike about yourself, you foster

stronger interpersonal bonds. Recognising and understanding your own unconscious patterns and projections contributes to more genuine and authentic connections with those around you.

- **Self-awareness and self-acceptance –** Exploring your shadow reveals hidden or denied aspects of yourself, making a vital stride in personal growth. Confronting activated shadow parts helps overcome insecurities, fostering greater self-compassion. Embracing your shadow becomes a pathway to releasing shame and cultivating a mindset free of self-hate.
- **Empowerment –** The integration of your shadow empowers you to assume responsibility for all facets of your life. Instead of being governed by subconscious forces, you cultivate a heightened sense of agency and control. Striking a balance between your conscious and subconscious aspects fosters a more harmonious life, paving the way for holistic and integrated experiences of the self.

As we conclude this chapter, take a moment to contemplate how your shadow impacts your healing.

- What have you learned?
- How are you going to implement this?

Chapter 13

Healing Your Shadow Self

Embarking on a journey of healing your shadow self involves exploring and integrating the unconscious facets of your personality. Consider these steps to guide you in engaging with and understanding your shadow:

Self-Reflection

Begin self-refection by contemplating your emotions, reactions and behaviours. Recognise reoccurring patterns and situations that evoke strong emotional responses. Pay close attention to these intense reactions, as they signify aspects of your shadow in need of exploration. Incorporating mindfulness and meditation can enhance awareness of your thoughts and emotions, providing a non-judgemental space for self-discovery.

journal

Maintain a journal to document your thoughts, feelings and observations. The act of writing serves as a potent tool, offering a valuable insight into your subconscious processes.

Journal prompts that will help are:

- What situations or individuals trigger strong emotional reactions in you? How do you respond to these triggers and why?
- Reflect on recurring patterns in your life, whether in relationships, work or personal habits. What themes or behaviours seem to repeat and what might they reveal about your shadow?
- How do your significant childhood memories influence your current beliefs, behaviours or fears?
- List qualities about yourself that you find uncomfortable or challenging. Explore where they might originate and how they manifest in your life.
- Explore any positive qualities within your shadow? How can you nurture these and integrate them into your conscious self?
- Reflect on your interactions with others, are there aspects of yourself that you tend to project onto others? Or are there aspects that you hide?
- How do your fears impact your decisions, relationships or self-esteem?

Other activities that might help are:

- Write a compassionate letter to yourself, acknowledging and accepting the parts of you that find challenging.
- Set goals for integrating aspects of your shadow into your conscious awareness.

Dream Analysis

According to Carl Jung, dreams offer a glimpse into the unconscious. Take note of reoccurring themes or symbols in your dreams and delve into their meanings.

How can you effectively analyse your dreams?

- **Keep a dream journal** - Maintain a dream journal by promptly recording details such as people, places, objects and emotions upon waking. Pay special attention to strong feelings or recurring themes.
- **Identify key symbols** - Identify key symbols within your dreams including objects, animals, people or places. Reflect on their personal significance to gain deeper insights.
- **Explore emotions** - Explore the emotions experienced during the dream, as they provide valuable clues to your subconscious feelings.

- **Recognise patterns** – Recognise patterns by observing reoccurring themes or motifs in your dreams, as these highlight unresolved issues or persistent thoughts in your waking life.
- **Analyse over time** – Conduct a long-term analysis of your dreams to identify reoccurring symbols or themes. Persistent patterns across dreams indicate significant aspects within your shadow.

Artistic Expression

Partake in creative activities such as art, play, writing or music; these outlets serve as powerful tools to express and explore aspects of your unconscious that are challenging to articulate verbally. One practice I follow is maintaining a drawing journal, where I create an intuitive drawing every day, relying solely on my intuition. This ritual enables me to establish a connection with my unconscious mind.

Embrace Vulnerability and Self-Compassion

Cultivate the willingness to acknowledge and sit with uncomfortable emotions. Embracing vulnerability empowers you to confront aspects of your shadow without judgement. Navigate this process with self-compassion. Recognise that everyone possesses a shadow and addressing it is a natural facet of personal growth; approach it without self-blame or criticism.

Face Your Fears

Confront your fears and insecurities consciously. Explore the root cause behind your fears and reflect on past experiences that have contributed to them. As you face and comprehend these aspects of yourself, you initiate the process of integrating them into your conscious awareness.

Cultivate Self-Acceptance

Cultivate self-acceptance, encompassing both the desirable and less favourable aspects. Acknowledge that these elements are inherent to being human and embracing them is a vital step towards integration. Identify positive qualities within your shadow self, such as creativity or assertiveness, and consciously incorporate them into your overall self-awareness.

As we conclude this chapter, take a moment to contemplate how your shadow self impacts you and how you can work towards healing.

- What have you learned?
- How will you implement it?

Part 2

Understanding Family Influences

Chapter 14

Mothers

The Role of the Mother

Mothers or mother figures hold a substantial and diverse influence in the lives of their children, with significance spanning personal, emotional, social and cultural dimensions. This relationship is frequently the initial and deepest emotional connection individuals establish, with mothers commonly serving as primary caregivers during their child's early years. They provide crucial care, nourishment, and emotional support, fostering the growth and development of children both physically and emotionally. The bond between mother and child plays a pivotal role in shaping an individual's emotional well-being and interpersonal relationships across their lifetime.

It is crucial to acknowledge that motherhood transcends biological or primary caregiving roles, encompassing various forms such as adoptive mothers, surrogate mothers, foster mothers, stepmothers and other maternal figures. The significance of mothers extends beyond biological and gender-based ties, encompassing those who assume maternal roles and responsibilities. It's essential to recognise diverse family structures, like my own, where my daughters have two mothers. We'll delve into these variations later on.

For the purpose of this chapter, I am using the term mother to refer to a child's primary caregiver. I am aware that mother is a gendered term and that the gender of a primary caregiver is not necessarily female, or any binary gender, and that families take many different shapes.

Key facets of the role of a mother are:

- Act as influential role models for their children, who often turn to them for guidance on values, behaviours and interpersonal relationships. A mother's conduct and choices hold significant sway in shaping a child's moral compass.
- Play a vital role in a child's early education by assisting in the development of language skills, cognitive abilities and social awareness. This foundational guidance lays the groundwork for a child's lifelong learning journey.
- Consistently serve as a pillar of emotional support and comfort throughout their child's life. Offering encouragement, understanding and a safe space, they create an environment where children feel free to express their feelings and thoughts.

- Contribute to security and stability, creating a stable and supportive environment that nurtures a child's sense of safety and well-being.
- Instil confidence, self-esteem and a strong sense of self-worth, equipping children with the skills and mindset necessary to confront life's challenges.
- Champion and safeguard the rights and well-being of their children, acting as advocates within their families and communities to ensure the fulfilment of their children's needs.
- Balance their roles as caregivers with various other needs and responsibilities, exemplifying resilience and equilibrium for their children.
- A mother's love is distinguished by its unconditional nature, establishing a bedrock of acceptance and unwavering support.

TYPES OF MOTHERS

Arguably, there are five distinct types of mothers, with various authors, psychologists and experts contributing to popularising these classifications. Each is characterised by the interactions and relationships they share with their children. Gaining insights into how you were mothered and how you approach motherhood yourself allows you to take meaningful steps towards healing.

The Perfectionist Mother

A perfectionist mother is characterised by a fervent pursuit of flawlessness and a determined commitment to uphold high standards, not only for herself but for her children. While striving for excellence can have positive aspects, perfectionism introduces stress, forges unrealistic expectations and poses challenges to the parent-child relationship.

My client, Maisie, presented in therapy with a perfectionist mother, with her mother setting a high bar and striving to keep up appearances. An example Maisie gave me was that when she was a child of around seven, she cut the fringe of a friend. Her mother was so embarrassed that her reaction was hugely disproportionate to the actions of Maisie. She berated Maisie to the point that Maisie was inconsolable. Her Mother was unable to offer any comfort. This left Maisie feeling rejected and unloved.

Key characteristics of perfectionist mothers include:

High Expectations and Fear of Failure: The perfectionist mother establishes exceedingly high standards not only for herself but for her children and their accomplishments. She might perceive anything less than perfection as unacceptable. Coping with imperfections and setbacks can be particularly challenging for these mothers, leading to responses of frustration, disappointment or self-criticism. A profound fear of failure is present, prompting the perfectionist mother to go to great lengths to avoid mistakes or any perceived shortfall in meeting her standards.

Micromanagement: Perfectionist mothers frequently involve themselves in micromanagement, meticulously overseeing and controlling various facets of their children's lives, spanning academics to extracurricular activities. Delegating tasks can pose a challenge for a perfectionist mother, as they firmly believe that they are the sole individual capable of meeting the high standards she has set.

Focus on External Validation: The perfectionist mother is inclined towards seeking external validation and approval, often tethering her sense of self-worth to both her own and her children's achievements. Consistently comparing her children to others, the perfectionist gauges their success against external benchmarks, inadvertently fostering a competitive environment.

Emphasis on Appearance: The perfectionist mother places a high value on appearance, both in terms of physical appearance and the portrayal of a perfect family. Striving to present an idealised image to others, perfectionist mothers densely schedule their children's activities and commitments, aiming for a well-rounded and successful upbringing.

Maisie described her mother as being focused on what other people thought and how they were perceived as a family.

Conditional Love: Love and approval within the realm of perfectionist mothers hinges on achieving specific milestones or meeting particular expectations. Children in such environments perceive their worth as intricately linked to their accomplishments.

Maisie described feeling that her mother's love was conditional on her behaving in a certain way and that if she didn't, she would be criticised or would feel that love had been withdrawn.

Anxiety and Stress: Perfectionism can contribute to elevated levels of anxiety and stress for both the mother and child; the relentless pursuit of perfection is demanding and exhausting. Finding relaxation and downtime will be challenging for the perfectionist mother as there is always a sense of urgency to accomplish more or perfect existing achievements.

Strained Relationships: The relentless pursuit of perfection can strain familial relationships, with children often lacking autonomy and possibly rebelling against the imposed standards. The pressure to meet unrealistic expectations instigates feelings of anxiety, self-doubt and a constant fear of failure among children.

THE IMPACT OF A PERFECTIONIST MOTHER

The influence of having a perfectionist mother during childhood can manifest in diverse ways during adulthood. Although not everyone raised by this type of mother will encounter identical outcomes, certain patterns and effects are frequently observed. These include:

High Achievement Orientation and Fear of Failure: Those of you raised by perfectionist mothers often adopt an orientation towards achievement. You harbour a perpetual drive to excel in diverse aspects of life, including career, academics, or personal goals. A lingering fear of failure persists into adulthood, deterring you from taking risks or pursuing new opportunities due to an entrenched apprehension of falling short of high standards or facing potential criticism.

Perfectionism in Relationships: Perfectionist tendencies can extend to your interpersonal relationships, you will set unrealistically high standards for yourself and your partners, resulting in dissatisfaction and strained relationships.

Low Self-Esteem: Being raised by a perfectionist mother can contribute to low self-esteem, persistent feelings of inadequacy and a constant sense of falling short of expectations. The pursuit of external validation can endure into adulthood, as you continue seeking approval and affirmation from others, anchoring your self-worth to external achievements. You find it challenging to handle criticism, even when constructive, often internalising it as a personal failure. This internalisation can lead to heightened sensitivity and defensiveness.

Procrastination or Avoidance: You can adopt procrastination or avoidance behaviours as a coping mechanism for the fear of not meeting perfectionist standards. This tendency can impede both personal and professional growth.

Maisie described that she adopted a “why bother trying” attitude towards achievement. She felt that she was capable of a lot more than she had yet achieved, but having such a fear of failure and a fear of what people would think if she did fail, led to strong avoidance behaviours and only approaching things that she knew she could succeed at.

Difficulty Relaxing: The perpetual need for achievement and perfection will give rise to challenges in relaxing or taking breaks. You experience guilt when not actively working towards goals or meeting expectations. The relentless pursuit of perfection can lead to overcommitment and a continuous drive for goals, potentially resulting in burnout.

Balancing work, personal life and self-care is particularly challenging for adults raised by perfectionist mothers. Establishing healthy boundaries, saying no, or prioritising your needs over others’ expectations can be a struggle for those of you shaped by the influence of perfectionism.

Impact on Parenting: Perfectionistic tendencies can significantly influence parenting styles. Adults raised by perfectionist mothers unintentionally pass on high standards and expectations to their own children, perpetuating the cycle.

Whilst many of these traits seem uncomfortable, they contribute to a strong sense of commitment in relationships. You will exhibit a remarkable sense of responsibility and reliability in everything you undertake.

Additionally, you place great value on hard work and persistence, considering them core character qualities.

The Unpredictable Mother

The unpredictable mother is defined by a state of overwhelm, often displaying anxiety, anger or excessive emotional reactions. Her parenting style revolves solely around her mood, making her the most chaotic among the five mother types. This mother tends to generate problems, issues and crises within her own mind, driven by her emotions and relationships, subsequently imparting them to her children.

The behaviour of an unpredictable mother can cultivate an environment of uncertainty and instability in her children. This unpredictability can manifest in diverse ways, significantly affecting a child's emotional well-being and sense of security.

Key aspects associated with unpredictable mothers include:

Mood Swings: An unpredictable mother will undergo frequent and intense mood swings, which presents a challenge for her children to anticipate her emotional state. Children raised by unpredictable mothers find themselves on an emotional rollercoaster, uncertain about what to expect in terms of love, approval or emotional support. Common traits include impulsive decision-making and actions, contributing to an environment where stability and routine are notably lacking.

Erratic Parenting: The approach to discipline in this parenting style can be erratic, swinging between permissive and strict without clear rules or boundaries. Children under such parenting find it challenging to comprehend the consequences of their actions due to inconsistent rules, expectations and levels of involvement.

The household, under erratic parenting, often lacks a consistent routine or structure, resulting in a prevailing sense of chaos and instability. The mother's reactions to various situations can be unpredictable, making it difficult for her children to gauge how she will respond. Furthermore, the mother's availability for emotional support or practical needs fluctuates, with moments of intense emotional presence followed by periods of seeming distant or preoccupied.

Unstable Relationships: The mother's relationships are unpredictable, characterised by frequent changes in friendships or romantic partners. This instability can affect the child's sense of stability.

THE IMPACT OF AN UNPREDICTABLE MOTHER

Similar to any parenting style, the effects extend into adulthood, shaping various aspects of your life. These outcomes are subjective, common manifestations include:

Difficulty Trusting: Navigating trust becomes a formidable task for those whose upbringing involved unpredictable maternal figures. The absence of reliability and consistency in early relationships can present formidable hurdles to establishing secure and trusting connections in adulthood. As I've mentioned previously, the repercussions of unpredictable parenting extend to the realm of attachment types, with adults potentially manifesting either anxious or avoidance patterns. These patterns significantly influence how you approach and navigate relationships, shaping the dynamics of your interpersonal interactions.

Fear of Rejection or Abandonment: the inherent unpredictability experienced during childhood can foster a lasting apprehension towards rejection or abandonment. Those of you who have experienced such an upbringing might find yourself highly attuned to perceived signals of rejection and grapple with persistent feelings of inadequacy. Additionally, you exhibit a recurrent tendency to seek approval and validation from others. This behavioural pattern is rooted in the irregular approval and emotional support you encountered from your unpredictable maternal figure, shaping your ongoing quest for reassurance and acknowledgement in adulthood.

Emotional Dysregulation: This becomes a significant hurdle for those of you raised in unpredictable environments, resulting in difficulties with effectively managing emotions. As adults, you find yourself struggling with stress management, often susceptible to heightened emotional responses.

The struggle to establish and adhere to routines in adulthood is a noteworthy manifestation of this challenge. This difficulty in maintaining structures and routines can exert its impact across various domains of life, influencing aspects such as work, relationships and self-care.

Relationship Challenges: Navigating relationships poses a formidable challenge for those of you who grew up amidst unpredictable parenting. The repercussions are evident in difficulties related to communication, intimacy and conflict resolution. The unpredictability of maternal figures hinders the development of effective expression of needs and boundaries within relationships, as you will have learned to adapt constantly to your mother's unpredictable needs. This adaptive behaviour can manifest in the form of perfectionist tendencies or engaging in people-pleasing behaviours as mechanisms to navigate the uncertainties of your environment and gain a sense of control. Consequently, expressing your needs and setting boundaries in relationships prove difficult given the ingrained pattern of continuous adaptation to the unpredictable needs of the maternal figure.

Coping Mechanisms: Coping mechanisms, such as hypervigilance or avoidance, can be forged in response to an unpredictable maternal influence and can endure into adulthood, shaping the way you navigate stress and uncertainty. These adaptive strategies, honed in response to the unpredictability of your mother, continue to influence how you cope with the challenges of adulthood, and whilst they have served you well during childhood, this is not always the case when you're an adult.

Self-Esteem: Navigating self-esteem can be a challenge, given the backdrop of inconsistent validation and approval that have characterised your upbringing. The fluctuating patterns of acknowledgement and approval contribute to struggles with self-worth, creating a complex terrain for developing a stable and positive sense of your own value.

Career Choices: The absence of stability and predictability during childhood can cast a shadow on career choices and achievements in adulthood. Decision-making and goal-setting are areas of struggle for you, as the imprint of an uncertain upbringing leaves its mark on your ability to navigate the professional landscape with confidence and clarity.

Whilst these observations lean towards negative aspects, it is essential to recognise the inherent resilience and adept coping skills that you will have cultivated. Your capacity to adapt to uncertainty not only shows your ability in problem-solving but positions you as someone with robust resilience. Furthermore, it's likely that you possess excellent interpersonal skills, marked by empathy, motivation and the ability to provide meaningful emotional support to others. These positive attributes bring a well-rounded set of strengths that have developed alongside the challenges you faced.

The Best Friend Mother

The mother who assumes the role of a best friend tends to blur traditional parent-child boundaries, preferring an approach where both parties are regarded as equals. In this dynamic, the responsibilities of setting boundaries are overlooked, creating a scenario where the parent and child find themselves occupying roles of emotional confidante and partner interchangeably. The mother, in turn, relies on the child to fulfil her emotional needs, contributing to an atypical parent-child relationship.

The best friend mother intentionally creates a close, supportive and friendship-based bond with her children, emphasising open communication and shared interests. Striving to play dual roles as both a parent and a friend, she aims to forge an environment of understanding and camaraderie. Key characteristics of this parenting style include:

Open Communication: Open and sincere communication is a hallmark of the best friend mother's parenting style. Establishing a foundation of trust, she encourages her children to freely express their thoughts and emotions without fear or judgement. This nurturing environment assures unconditional support and provides a space where children feel at ease confiding in her, confident that guidance will be offered without criticism. The best friend mother and her children share a sense of confidentiality, creating a safe haven where personal thoughts and secrets can be shared.

However, a potential drawback arises when the mother excessively confides in her child, leading to an imbalance in the information shared. Despite this, the best friend mother remains committed to understanding her children's perspective, validating their emotions and demonstrating empathy and comprehension. Acting as the primary emotional support system, she becomes a go-to figure for comfort, advice and understanding. While this strengthens the bond between the best friend mother and her child, it could potentially result in less connected relationships with other caregivers.

With a vision of lifelong friendship, the best friend mother aims to see the parent-child relationship evolve and deepen over time, maintaining its role as a steadfast source of support and companionship.

Shared Interests: The best friend mother actively participates in shared interests and hobbies with her children, purposefully reinforcing their bond and establishing common ground for connection. Her willingness to engage in spontaneous activities injects an element of fun into the relationship, cultivating moments of joy and creating a reservoir of positive memories for both parent and child.

Respect for Autonomy: Demonstrating profound respect for the autonomy and individuality of her children, this mother navigates the delicate balance of offering guidance while recognising the significance of allowing her children to make their own choices and decisions. Even in adopting the role of a best friend, she remains aware of her parental responsibilities, skillfully maintaining equilibrium between friendship and providing essential guidance.

The best friend mother displays an adaptive parenting style, attuned to the evolving needs of her children. Acknowledging the inherent changes that accompany their growth, she embraces flexibility in response to the shifting dynamics of their relationship.

THE IMPACT OF A BEST FRIEND MOTHER

The influence of having a best friend mother during childhood can manifest in diverse ways. Primarily, this close and supportive relationship tends to yield positive outcomes. However, it is equally important to acknowledge and consider potential challenges. Impacts include:

Positive Communication: Those of you who had a best friend mother often develop a comfort in expressing yourself openly and honestly. This upbringing not only fosters your own emotional articulation but enhances your ability to comprehend and respond to the emotional expressions of others. As a result, you are likely to exhibit a high degree of emotional intelligence.

Strong Bonds: Those of you raised by a best friend mother often excel in forming robust connections in your adult relationships. Approaching relationships with a friend-oriented mindset, you will display adaptability and navigate changes with ease. Moreover, you are likely to feel at ease with emotional intimacy, fostering deep and meaningful connections with others.

Independence: The best friend mother's emphasis on autonomy can shape the child into an adult who highly values independence. This upbringing tends to cultivate self-reliance and a strong ability to make decisions autonomously.

Over-Identification: A potential challenge arises in the form of over-identification or enmeshment, where you encounter difficulties in establishing clear boundaries between the roles of a parent and a friend. This issue has the potential to significantly impact the cultivation of a healthy parent-child dynamic. Those of you affected might find it challenging to set and maintain healthy emotional boundaries, not only with your mothers but in other close relationships.

Challenges Recognising Authority: Those raised by a best friend mother face difficulties in recognising and respecting authority figures. The nature of this parenting style, which emphasises a more equal relationship, could contribute to a potential struggle in acknowledging traditional authority structures.

The Me-First Mother

Mothers with a me-first approach struggle to see their children as distinct individuals, often displaying self-absorption and insecurity. From an early age, their children learn that part of their role is to ensure that their mother takes the spotlight. This mother prioritises her own needs, desires, and well-being over those of her children. Defining aspects of this mother type include:

Self-Centred Orientation: The me-first mother is characterised by a self-centred focus, placing her own needs at the forefront. Her primary concern revolves around fulfilling personal goals and aspirations. Consequently, she often exhibits limited empathy for the emotional needs and desires of her child. Her actions and decisions are driven by what serves her interests, rather than prioritising what is best for her children. The pursuit of personal fulfilment will lead this mother to engage in career goals, hobbies or personal relationships without fully considering the potential impact on her children.

Potential Neglect of Children's Needs: The offspring of a me-first mother encounter neglect or inconsistent attention, as this mother tends to be preoccupied with her own pursuits. The singular focus on personal goals can result in a lack of consistent emotional support for the children. The me-first mother faces challenges in providing stability, as routine and consistent caregiving is compromised due to her devotion to personal pursuits.

IMPACT OF THE ME-FIRST MOTHER

The impact of having a me-first mother during childhood can manifest in various ways. While the self-centred orientation of this parenting style poses challenges, it is crucial to recognise both its positive and negative outcomes. Acknowledging the potential drawbacks is essential in understanding the complex dynamics that shape those of you raised by a me-first mother. Impacts include:

Difficulty Prioritising Needs: Those of you who were raised by a me-first mother encounter challenges in prioritising your own needs and desires. Early exposure to a self-centred parental influence can shape your ability to establish healthy boundaries and prioritise self-care.

The absence of consistent boundaries during childhood impacts your capacity to assert yourself and set limits effectively. As a response, you overcompensate by consistently putting others' needs before your own and displaying self-sacrificing behaviours. This tendency will originate from a desire to avoid replicating the self-centred dynamics experienced in childhood.

On the other hand, you can adopt a pursuit of independence and autonomy as a coping mechanism to navigate the lack of consistent emotional support during your younger years.

Relationship Challenges: The influence of a me-first mother can manifest in challenges when navigating relationships. You grapple with the delicate balance between meeting your own needs and attending to the needs of others, potentially resulting in difficulties forming and sustaining healthy connections. Fear of intimacy or hesitancy to fully engage emotionally in close relationships is apparent, stemming from the lack of consistent emotional availability experienced during childhood. This early emotional landscape can contribute to hurdles in forming deep and intimate connections in adulthood.

Those raised by a me-first mother encounter uncertainty in their own approach to parenting. Struggling to reconcile personal fulfilment with the responsibilities of parenthood, you find it challenging to strike a harmonious balance between your individual needs and the demands of being a parent. This inner conflict can pose additional layers of complexity to your journey in building and maintaining meaningful family connections.

Seeking External Validation: Those of you brought up by a me-first mother develop a tendency to seek external validation, driven by the absence of consistent emotional support in childhood. Compensating for the lack of validation at home, you actively look for approval and recognition from others to fill the void left by these deficiencies in childhood.

You grapple with self-esteem challenges, carrying the burden of feelings of inadequacy or unworthiness due to the inconsistent affirmation and support you received. Doubts about your own decision-making abilities persist, making it difficult for you to trust your feelings on any matter. This struggle often stems from a historical pattern of prioritising your mother's opinion over your own, reinforcing a sense that external validation holds more weight than your internal compass.

Struggle with Empathy: For those raised by mothers primarily focused on their own needs, empathy can pose a notable challenge. Understanding and connecting with the emotions of others prove difficult as the emphasis on your mother's self-centred approach will have hindered the development of a nuanced and empathic understanding of your feelings and the feelings of those around you.

Coping Mechanisms: In response to the self-centred parenting style, you have developed specific coping mechanisms. These strategies can involve emotional withdrawal, building self-reliance, or using defensive behaviours as protective measures against potential emotional neglect.

On the positive side, you excel in supporting others, displaying exceptional intuition and insight in various types of relationships. Your loyalty and supportiveness stand out, allowing you to genuinely appreciate the needs of those around you and effectively solve problems in a considerate manner.

The Complete Mother

The complete mother seamlessly integrates the most positive aspects of the other four mother types. Emotionally balanced, she possesses the ability to view her children as unique individuals and actively supports them in attaining their independence. Acknowledging that perfection is unattainable, she remains committed to the journey of motherhood, navigating its challenges with dedication and resilience, regardless of her emotional circumstances.

Defining aspects of the complete mother are:

Balanced Nurturing: The complete mother excels at cultivating a harmonious and nurturing environment for her children. She seamlessly blends emotional support, love and care with a strong sense of responsibility, guiding her children with empathy even when administering discipline. Recognising the importance of setting boundaries and enforcing rules, she does so with a keen understanding of the emotional well-being of her children.

Prioritising stability and routine, this mother creates an environment that brings a sense of security to her children. Consistency in daily life not only fosters predictability but contributes to a nurturing atmosphere. Ensuring her children feel safe, loved and supported is a paramount goal for the complete mother, laying the foundation for their healthy emotional development.

Individuality and Independence: The complete mother not only recognises but actively encourages the importance of individuality, motivating her children to explore their interests and cultivate a sense of independence. Striking a delicate balance, she provides unwavering support for their personal growth while ensuring a secure foundation. As a positive role model, the complete mother embodies qualities such as empathy, resilience, kindness and responsibility, imparting invaluable life lessons to her children.

Proactively engaging in their development, she teaches essential life skills, including problem-solving, decision-making, and practical tasks, equipping her children with the necessary tools to navigate the complexities of life. While offering steadfast support, the complete mother fosters independence by allowing her children to take age-appropriate risks and responsibilities, nurturing self-reliance.

In her quest to foster holistic development, the complete mother instils a love for learning and cultivates curiosity in her children. Wholeheartedly supporting their educational endeavours, she creates an environment where learning is not only encouraged but deeply valued.

Emotional Availability: Consistently exemplifying emotional availability, the complete mother creates an environment where her children feel secure approaching her with concerns. They trust that she will not only listen but understand and provide unwavering support. Open communication is a cornerstone of the complete mother's parenting style, as she actively encourages her children to freely express their thoughts and feelings. This commitment to fostering open dialogue establishes an atmosphere of trust and understanding, fortifying the emotional connection between the mother and her children. The complete mother will encourage her children to feel their feelings, fully experience and sit with their emotions, rather than avoiding or repressing them.

Adaptability: The complete mother demonstrates remarkable adaptability, recognising that as her children grow and develop, her parenting approach must evolve to meet their changing needs.

Celebrating Achievements: In the complete mother's household, the practice of celebrating achievements – both big and small – is a standard, fostering a positive and encouraging environment that acknowledges and uplifts her children's accomplishments.

Unconditional Love: At the heart of this parenting style is unconditional love. Children parented this way will feel a profound sense of security, knowing they are loved and accepted for who they are, creating a foundation for their emotional well-being and self-assurance.

THE IMPACT OF THE COMPLETE MOTHER

Though individual impacts vary, there are several ways that the positive influence of a complete mother might manifest in adulthood.

Healthy Relationship Patterns: Those of you raised by a complete mother often demonstrate healthy relationship patterns in adulthood. You are adept at forming secure attachments and navigating intimate relationships with a solid foundation of trust and open communication.

You will tend to possess effective communication skills, as the encouragement of open communication during childhood translates into your ability to express thoughts and feelings clearly and empathically.

The complete mother's support for emotional expression fosters comfort with vulnerability. As an adult, you are more open to sharing your authentic self with others and embracing vulnerability, not as a weakness but as a strength in building meaningful connections.

Emotional Resilience: The unwavering emotional support offered by this mother type plays a pivotal role in fostering emotional resilience in adulthood. Individuals raised in such an environment are well-equipped to navigate life's challenges and setbacks with strength and resilience.

Positive Self-Esteem: The nurturing environment fostered by a complete mother significantly contributes to the development of positive self-esteem. Those of you who have experienced unconditional love and unwavering support during your early years often possess a robust sense of self-worth.

Those raised by a complete mother frequently prioritise self-care. Your understanding of the importance of overall well-being and a nurturing environment instils in you a commitment to maintaining physical, emotional and mental health throughout your life.

Balance: A complete mother adeptly fosters independence whilst offering a secure foundation. In adulthood, those of you raised in this environment often show a healthy balance between autonomy and connection, feeling confident in your ability to navigate life independently yet maintaining meaningful connections with others.

The adaptability of a complete mother to changing needs significantly shapes you to embody adaptability and flexibility in various aspects of life. You will tend to be open to new experiences and can navigate transitions effectively, demonstrating resilience in the face of change.

The overall positive and supportive environment cultivated by a complete mother will contribute to your positive outlook on life. In the face of challenges, you will approach situations with resilience and maintain a hopeful perspective, reflecting the enduring impact of your nurturing upbringing.

Parenting Skills: Those of you raised by a complete mother often exhibit effective parenting skills. Drawing on your own positive experiences, you strive to create a nurturing environment for your own children, emphasising emotional support, consistent discipline and open communication.

Emotional Intelligence: The cultivation of emotional expression and understanding during childhood paves the way for heightened emotional intelligence in adulthood. If you experienced this encouragement, you tend to be finely attuned to both your own emotions and those of others.

Lifelong Learning: The emphasis on learning and curiosity instilled during childhood often translates into a pursuit of lifelong learning in adulthood. If you were raised in this way, you will frequently exhibit a keen interest in both personal and professional development.

Boundaries: The demonstration of healthy boundary-setting in childhood often leads to adults who are proficient at establishing and maintaining healthy boundaries in their relationships and personal lives.

As we conclude this chapter, take a moment to contemplate how your mother has impacted you.

- What have you learned?
- How are you going to implement this?

Chapter 15

Healing From Your Mothering Experience

Navigating the healing process from any type of mothering experience entails acknowledging the positive aspects of your upbringing while actively addressing any challenges or lingering effects. Consider incorporating the following strategies to aid in this healing journey:

Reflection

Allocate time for thoughtful reflection on your experiences and recognise the profound impact your mother has had on your beliefs and behaviours. Assess your own values and aspirations independently of external expectations. Contemplate what matters to you and align your goals with your authentic self. Then set realistic and achievable goals, breaking larger aspirations into manageable steps for a more achievable path forward.

In the course of reflection, pay attention to patterns and triggers that evoke memories of your upbringing. Understanding these patterns empowers you to respond differently in the present, fostering personal growth and resilience. Explore whether your emotional needs were met by your mother or identify areas where support was lacking. It is crucial to acknowledge and validate your feelings about your childhood to provide a foundation for emotional healing and self-acceptance.

Establish and Maintain Healthy Boundaries

Cultivate the skill of setting and maintaining healthy boundaries in your relationships. Articulate your needs clearly and prioritise self-care without harbouring guilt. Develop assertiveness in expressing limits, ensuring that your boundaries are respected.

Hold realistic expectations for both yourself and others. Embrace the understanding that perfection is unattainable and recognise that everyone is on their own unique path. Release the pressure to meet impossible standards and shift your focus from perfection to progress. Understand that growth and development are continual processes and celebrate the journey rather than fixating on an idealised destination.

Seek Support

Don't hesitate to reach out to family and friends when you need it. Engaging in open conversations about your experiences and feelings with someone you trust can offer valuable validation and perspective. Surround yourself with people who genuinely support and uplift you. Cultivate a network of relationships that provide authenticity, personal growth and self-compassion. Building this kind of supportive community can be instrumental in your healing journey.

Forgiveness and Self-Compassion

In your healing journey, consider embracing forgiveness as a transformative process. This doesn't mean condoning negative experiences or poor behaviours but rather, it entails letting go of resentments to find peace for your own well-being. Acceptance is a key facet of forgiveness; understand that your mother is likely to be acting out her own mother wounds.

Practice self-compassion by treating yourself with kindness and understanding. Acknowledge that your responses to your mother were adaptive mechanisms and recognise that you deserve love and care.

Explore your emotional needs. Understand what is essential for you to feel supported and fulfilled. This heightened awareness serves as a guide in forming healthier connections and meeting your own emotional needs, fostering a more fulfilling life.

Build empathy towards both yourself and others. Recognise that everyone carries unique strengths and challenges. This understanding not only fosters self-compassion but strengthens interpersonal relationships, creating a foundation for more meaningful connections.

Invest time in developing your own self-identity. Explore your interests, values and aspirations. Rediscover who you are outside the influence of your mother and actively nurture your individuality. This process allows you to reclaim your autonomy and embrace the fullness of your authentic self.

Mindfulness

Incorporate mindfulness and meditation into your routine to cultivate a present and non-judgmental awareness. These techniques empower you to observe your thoughts and emotions without becoming overwhelmed by them, fostering a sense of balance and clarity.

Engage in the imaginative exercise of parenting yourself with the same compassion and understanding you needed as a child. Extend to yourself the love and care that you deserve, promoting a nurturing and healing relationship with your own inner self.

Healing From A Perfectionist Mother

Challenging Unrealistic Beliefs

Begin by identifying and challenging any unrealistic or harmful beliefs about perfection that you have internalised. Replace these beliefs with more realistic and compassionate perspectives. Build self-compassion by treating yourself with kindness and understanding, recognising that it's perfectly acceptable not to be perfect.

Pay close attention to any negative self-talk and perfectionist thoughts that arise. Actively challenge and reframe these thoughts by substituting them with positive and affirming statements. By consistently challenging these patterns you foster a healthier mindset that embraces progress over perfection.

Set Realistic Expectations

Set realistic and achievable goals for yourself. Break down larger tasks into smaller, more manageable steps, and celebrate your progress at every milestone along the way.

Cultivate a growth mindset that views challenges and failures as valuable opportunities for learning and improvement. Shift your focus from fixating on outcomes to valuing the ongoing process of growth. By adopting this perspective, you forge a resilient and forward-thinking approach to your personal and professional development.

Embrace Your Imperfections

Welcome your imperfections as an inherent aspect of the human experience. Recognise that making mistakes does not diminish your worth; instead, it offers valuable opportunities for growth and learning.

Healing from the influence of a perfectionist mother is a gradual process that entails self-discovery, self-acceptance and intentional efforts to change ingrained patterns. Be patient with yourself and understand that healing is an ongoing journey towards greater self-awareness and well-being. Remember that each step you take is a meaningful stride towards a healthier and more fulfilling life.

journal

Journal prompts to help you to heal from a perfectionist mother are as follows:

- What are early memories you have of your mother's expectations and standards? How did these early experiences shape your beliefs about perfection?
- Reflect on the beliefs about perfection that you have inherited from your mother. How do these beliefs influence your thoughts and behaviours today?
- How has your mother's perfectionism influenced your self-esteem and self-worth? Explore any positive or negative impacts on your confidence and sense of identity.

- Did your mother encourage comparisons or competition with others? How has this influenced your own tendencies to compare yourself to others or be competitive?
- How do you navigate the pursuit of success? Are there any patterns from your upbringing that you see in your goal-setting process?
- Explore any fears or anxieties you have about failure. How does the fear of not meeting expectations or making mistakes manifest in your life?
- Reflect on whether you tended to rebel or comply with your mother's standards. How has this dynamic influenced your life choices and relationships?

Healing From an Unpredictable Mother

Validation

Take the time to acknowledge and validate the array of emotions you experienced as a result of your unpredictable upbringing. It's perfectly okay to feel a range of emotions and recognising them is a crucial component of the healing process. Throughout this journey, treat yourself with kindness and understanding. Acknowledge that your responses to unpredictability were adaptive mechanisms and affirm to yourself that you deserve love and care during this transformative period of self-discovery and healing.

Reframe Negative Self-Talk

Actively challenge and reframe negative self-talk by replacing critical thoughts with positive and affirming statements. Shift your focus towards recognising your strengths and celebrating your achievements. This intentional change in perspective contributes to fostering a healthier and more positive mindset.

Emotional Regulation

Invest time in developing emotional regulation skills by incorporating mindfulness, deep breathing or other relaxation techniques into your routine to effectively manage stress and emotional responses. Introduce consistency and routine into your daily life wherever possible. Establish regular habits and routines to offer a valuable sense of stability and predictability, contributing to a more balanced emotional well-being.

Acknowledge that the healing journey is a gradual process, and therefore, practice patience and self-kindness along the way.

journal

- How would you describe your experiences with your mother during childhood? What were the more challenging aspects?
- What emotions arise when you think about your relationship with your unpredictable mother? Allow yourself to feel and express them without judgement?
- Consider how your experiences with your mother has influenced your adult relationships. Are there patterns or behaviours that you notice?
- Reflect on the positive traits you've developed as a result of navigating an unpredictable childhood. How have you demonstrated resilience and adaptability?
- Explore your experiences with setting and maintaining boundaries. In what areas of your life do you feel comfortable asserting your needs? And where do you struggle?
- Identify any negative thoughts or beliefs you hold about yourself due to your unpredictable upbringing. Challenge these thoughts and reframe in a more positive light.
- What steps can you take towards forgiveness and releasing emotional burdens?

Healing From a Best Friend Mother

Differentiate Roles

Acknowledge the distinct roles within your relationships. While the elements of friendships are valuable, recognise that parental roles involve guidance, structure and occasionally making decisions that don't align with your immediate desires. Foster a robust support network with diverse relationships, cultivating connections with individuals who provide varied perspectives and support different aspects of your life. This approach enhances the richness and depth of your social connections.

Address Enmeshment

If you recognise signs of enmeshment in your relationships, take steps to address them. Enmeshment can hinder your ability to form healthy boundaries and maintain individuality. This can include exploring new interests and activities outside of your typical shared experience, this can help you to develop your individual identity apart from the influence of your best friend mother. The information on healing from the enmeshment/underdeveloped self-schema in the earlier chapter will help with this.

journal

Journal prompts to help you heal from a best friend mother are as follows:

- Write about positive and enjoyable experiences you had with your mother. What moments stand out as affirming and supportive?
- Identify and acknowledge any challenges or difficulties you had with your mother. How did they impact you?
- Reflect on how your best friend mother supported your independence and autonomy. In what ways did this influence your ability to make decisions and navigate life?
- How have your experiences with your best friend mother influenced your approach to friendships and intimate relationships?
- Reflect how your best friend mother's parenting style influenced your sense of identity. How did it shape your self-perception and beliefs about who you are?

Explore Your Emotional Needs

Explore your emotional needs; identify and understand what is essential for you to feel supported and fulfilled. This heightened awareness becomes a guiding force in forming healthier connections and meeting your emotional needs autonomously.

Cultivate empathy towards both yourself and others by recognising the unique struggles and challenges everyone faces. This understanding serves as a foundation for fostering compassion, ultimately strengthening your interpersonal relationships.

Dedicate time to developing your self-identity. Explore your interests, values and aspirations to rediscover who you are beyond the influence of your mother. Actively nurture your individuality, fostering a deeper connection with your authentic self.

Positive Affirmations

Utilise affirmations to bolster positive beliefs about yourself. Develop and regularly repeat affirmations that reinforce your worth, strength and ability to overcome challenges. Consistent practice of these affirmations can contribute to fostering a more positive and empowering mindset.

journal

Journal prompts to reflect on and start healing from a me-first mother are:

- Acknowledge the impact of your me-first mother. What aspects stand out?
- Reflect on your emotional needs. How were they met or not met?
- Consider the boundaries (or lack of) in your relationships with your mother, how did they impact on your sense of self?
- Reflect on how your me-first mother's focus on her own needs influenced your sense of independence. In what ways did it shape your ability to make decisions for yourself?
- Affirm your self-worth independently of your me-first mother's actions. What positive qualities and strengths do you recognise in yourself?

Archetypes

It's essential to recognise that these five mother types are archetypes, and most mothers exhibit aspects of different types. I can recognise aspects of the perfectionist mother and the best friend mother in my own mum, and I can recognise aspects of all types within myself as a mother.

It's crucial to consider additional influences from various other family members and the environment in which you grew up. It's worth noting that when a father or other individual assumes the primary caregiver role, they can align with the categories discussed here. Similarly, in the next chapter, where I will delve into father archetypes, it's worth noting that a mother can also fit in to those roles.

As we come to the end of this chapter, take time to reflect on your own experience of being mothered and how it impacts on you in the here and now.

- What have you learned?
- How will you implement this?

Chapter 16

Fathers

The Importance of Fathers

Fathers play a pivotal and multifaceted role in the development and well-being of their children. While the role of a father differs from that of a mother, it spans across various dimensions, influencing emotional, social, cognitive and behavioural aspects of their child's life.

Contributing significantly to emotional development, fathers provide love, support and a sense of security. Positive father-child relationships cultivate emotional resilience, enabling children to navigate their feelings more effectively.

Acknowledging and endorsing the diverse roles that fathers play in their children's lives is crucial for fostering healthy family dynamics and overall child development. As I write this, I am keenly aware that my own children do not have a traditional father figure, instead they have two mothers. Nevertheless, I believe that everything I've written and am about to explore applies equally to the father figures or caregivers in a child's life regardless of gender.

Key facets of the father role are:

- Stimulating cognitive development through play, conversation and problem-solving. Fathers often bring a unique perspective and style of interaction that complements the mother's influence.
- Crucial in the development of social skills and the formation of healthy relationships. Positive interactions with fathers contribute to the child's ability to connect with others, develop empathy and navigate social situations.
- Fathers who are actively involved in their child's education and intellectual pursuits contribute to higher academic achievement.
- A supportive and stimulating home environment, including a father's encouragement, can positively impact educational outcomes.
- Contribute to the establishment of boundaries and the development of self-discipline in their child.
- Take on the role of disciplinarian, guiding children to understand and adhere to rules.
- Engage in activities that promote problem-solving skills and critical thinking. Their involvement in constructive play and shared activities encourages children to think independently and find solutions.

- Positive father-child relationships contribute to the development of resilience and effective coping mechanisms.
- Provide a source of support during challenging times, teaching children how to navigate difficulties.
- Introduce an element of adventure and risk-taking into a child's life. Through shared activities, fathers can teach children about calculated risks, courage and the importance of trying new things.
- Contribute to the formation of the child's identity by providing a sense of belonging and instilling a positive self-image.
- Helps children to build a strong foundation for a healthy self-concept.
- Their behaviours, attitudes and values shape children's understanding of what it means to be an adult, a partner and a contributing member of society.

Types of Fathers

Arguably there are five types of fathers. Reflecting on how you were fathered and examining the interactions between you and your father can be instrumental in the healing process.

The Angry Father

The angry father is not only disengaged; he is actively enraged. In the eyes of his children, he consistently appears angry or frustrated, and this anger manifests in hurtful words, tones and actions. The family will tread carefully, walking on eggshells around him due to the uncertainty of his reactions. It's crucial to recognise that anger is a complex emotion and individuals who exhibit anger do so for various reasons.

Key aspects of the angry father are:

- Expresses frustration easily even in response to minor issues. Small inconveniences or disruptions trigger his anger, frustration or impatience.
- Managing stress can be a challenge whether related to work, personal life or family matters, stress will escalate his emotional responses.
- Patience is in short supply, struggling to tolerate delays, mistakes or behaviours not in line with his expectations.
- Effective communication is a challenge, he has difficulty expressing his emotions or needs constructively.
- Emotional state can shift unexpectedly.
- Attempts to exert control over his family as a way of managing his own emotions, manifesting in rigid rules, expectations or a need for compliance.

- Anger serves as the default emotion, masking deeper feelings such as sadness or fear.

THE IMPACT OF THE ANGRY FATHER

The impact of having an angry father in childhood can manifest in diverse ways in adulthood. It's essential to acknowledge that individual experiences vary, and not everyone who grew up with an angry father or any type of parent will necessarily exhibit the described traits, Nevertheless, potential impacts include:

Emotional Challenges

Those of you who experienced an angry father during childhood encounter difficulties in regulating your own emotions, making it challenging to express and manage anger, consequently affecting your relationships. Coping strategies vary, from avoiding confrontation to exhibiting aggressive behaviour This can impact communication and conflict resolution skills and hinder the ability to establish healthy boundaries.

Furthermore, you may struggle to express a range of emotions, having learned to suppress feelings as a coping mechanism. This suppression makes it challenging to communicate effectively about your needs and emotions, affecting the depth of emotional expression.

The chronic stress and turmoil experienced in childhood contribute to depression or anxiety issues in adulthood, as the lingering impact of past experiences continues to affect emotional well-being.

Trust Issues

Growing up with an angry father can result in challenges when it comes to trusting others. Individuals approach forming close relationships with caution, fearing potential anger or conflict. This caution can extend to fear of intimacy, stemming from past experiences with an angry father, resulting in difficulties opening up emotionally and struggling with vulnerability in relationships.

Low Self-Esteem

Constant exposure to anger in childhood contributes to low self-esteem and feelings of inadequacy in adulthood. Those of you who experienced this environment grapple with self-worth issues, seeking external validation to compensate for these insecurities. Some develop perfectionist tendencies or engage in over-achievement as a means to gain approval or avoid triggering anger. However, the pursuit of success under such conditions comes at the cost of your own well-being.

The Absent Father

This father deliberately chooses not to be present in his children's lives. Although he played a role in bringing them into the world, he is currently not involved in their lives at all. His children won't even know who he is or where he can be found. The reasons for his absence vary – he might choose to stay away due to feelings of shame that make a return too challenging to face, or he may have other reasons influencing this decision.

Aspects of this father type are:

- Unreliable presence – intermittently involved or showing up sporadically with no way for the children to rely on his support.
- Leaves the remaining parent with the additional burden of responsibility. Siblings can experience differing levels of connection with the absent father.
- May provide financial support but no actual engagement.

THE IMPACT OF THE ABSENT FATHER

Ways that the impact of the absent father shows in adulthood are:

Relationships Challenges

Those with absent fathers encounter difficulties in forming and sustaining intimate relationships. They may have issues of trust, vulnerability and a fear of abandonment. These challenges can significantly affect your ability to connect with others on a deep emotional level.

Moreover, those of you with absent fathers can develop an insecure attachment type, further impacting your capacity to form healthy and secure connections in adulthood.

You experience a persistent longing for a paternal figure, influencing not only your adult relationships but your overall emotional well-being. This sense of longing contributes to complex dynamics in your relationship and emotional experiences.

Emotional Regulation

In adulthood, you encounter heightened emotional reactivity, mood swings, or difficulties expressing and managing your feelings effectively. Coping mechanisms developed in childhood, such as avoidance, emotional suppression, or reliance on maladaptive coping strategies, persist into adulthood. These patterns can impact emotional well-being and interpersonal relationships, requiring intentional efforts for healthy emotional regulation.

• • •

Low Self-Worth

The absence of a father figure can contribute to profound feelings of inadequacy and low self-esteem in adulthood. You question your inherent value and struggle with identity and self-worth. This absence leaves a lasting impact on your self-perception, necessitating efforts to cultivate a positive and resilient sense of self.

Trust Issues

Once more, those of you with absent fathers encounter challenges in trusting others, particularly authority figures. You exhibit wariness in hierarchical relationships, finding it difficult to accept guidance from mentors or supervisors. These trust issues can permeate various aspects of life, impacting professional and personal relationships, and require intentional efforts to build trust and establish positive connections.

The Emotionally Absent Father

While this father is physically present in the home, there is a noticeable emotional absence. Children see him, but engaging in meaningful conversation with him proves challenging. He often chooses to seclude himself away from the family or display emotional detachment from others in the home. Aspects characterising the emotionally absent father include:

- Struggling to express emotion, especially those related to vulnerability, love and empathy. He finds it challenging to connect with his children and avoids conversations about feelings and emotions which can create a barrier.
- Difficulty in understanding and responding to the emotions of his children is a challenge for the emotionally absent father. He lacks the ability to attune to their emotional needs.
- Affectionate gestures, such as hugs, kisses or verbal expressions of love are infrequent. He appears distant and reserved.
- Prioritises external achievements such as academic success over emotional wellbeing.

My client Jessica would describe her father as emotionally absent. This absence was displayed through his complete lack of affection, minimal emotional expression, and disregard for her own emotional cues. Jessica perceived that her father placed no value on her emotional well-being, often dismissing or ignoring her emotions. The emotional connection between them, in her view, was virtually non-existent.

THE IMPACT OF THE EMOTIONALLY ABSENT FATHER

Impacts of the emotionally absent father are:

Relationships Issues

Those of you who grew up with emotionally absent fathers encounter difficulties in forming and sustaining intimate relationships. Issues with trust, emotional vulnerability, and expressing your own emotions can result in emotional detachment, leading to a sense of isolation. Expressing emotions openly is a challenge, as you will have learned to suppress your feelings as a coping mechanism, contributing to difficulties in effective communication about emotional needs and a tendency to avoid emotional situations.

The fear of rejection and anxiety in relationships are heightened, influencing interactions and decision-making. Trust issues can play a part, with hesitancy to trust others due to concerns about potential disappointment or abandonment. Emotional intimacy might pose challenges, as individuals impacted by emotionally absent fathers find it difficult to share deeper emotions or connect with others on a profound emotional level.

Setting healthy boundaries in relationships is a struggle, as you can have difficulty asserting yourself. Bouncing back from setbacks or navigating life's challenges effectively presents challenges for those affected by the emotional absence of a father.

Jessica, for example, attended therapy due to a string of unhealthy relationships. She presented with great difficulty in setting and holding boundaries. She constantly feared rejection which resulted in people-pleasing behaviours.

Seeking Validation

The absence of emotional support from a father figure during childhood can result in a persistent need for validation from others in adulthood. Seeking external approval can be a way to compensate for the deficiency in emotional affirmation experienced earlier. This quest for validation manifests in various aspects of life.

You grapple with self-esteem and self-worth challenges, harbouring feelings of unimportance or being unworthy of love and affirmation. These feelings contribute to a sense of inadequacy that persists into adulthood.

Furthermore, there might be a tendency to develop perfectionist tendencies or engage in overachievement as a means to secure external validation. The relentless pursuit of success serves as an attempt to fill the emotional void created by the absent father, becoming a way to prove to yourself that you are worthy and significant.

Jessica described how she would constantly seek out reassurance from others and needed to be told that she was valuable. She described feeling a sense of inadequacy and she certainly talked about her perfectionist tendencies and her constant drive for success.

The Non-Residential Father

The non-residential father, often constrained by work commitments or family living arrangements, can find himself unable to spend full-time with his children. Despite potentially having good intentions or being a caring father, the limited time available for engagement with his children, through no choice of his own, falls short of their needs. This situation can lead to frustration for the father as he recognises the importance of spending more time with his children but faces practical constraints that hinder the desired level of involvement.

Aspects of this type of father are:

- Only present in the lives of his children part of the time
- Connection with children follows a specific routine.
- The non-residential father faces challenges in fulfilling daily parenting responsibilities due to limited time.
- Despite limited physical presence, the non-residential father will make efforts to stay connected through phone calls, video chats or other means of communication. He strives to

maintain a meaningful connection through periods of separation.

- The non-residential father prioritises the quality of time spent with his over the quantity, aiming to create meaningful and enjoyable experiences.
- Experiences feelings of guilt or frustration due to the constraints on his involvement.
- Navigates co-parenting dynamics with the children's other parent.

THE IMPACT OF THE NON-RESIDENTIAL FATHER

Impacts of the non-residential father are:

Emotional Well-being

If you grew up without a consistent father figure, you will encounter challenges in forming secure attachments in adulthood, affecting your ability to trust and connect with others emotionally. The absence of a positive male role model can contribute to feelings of inadequacy and low self-worth, potentially influencing decision-making, relationships and overall confidence.

Relationship Patterns

You will encounter difficulties in forming and sustaining intimate relationships, grappling with trust issues, fear or abandonment, or challenges in expressing emotions. You lack a clear understanding of how to navigate relationships.

Behavioural Patterns

You might find yourself adopting risky behaviours as a way to cope with any emotional emptiness. The impact manifests in externalising behaviours, such as occasional aggression or defiance, or internalising behaviours, like periods of withdrawal or feelings of depression.

The Active Father

Whilst no parent type is flawless, the active father is consistently emotionally present. He actively engages with, pays attention to, and makes himself available and accessible to his children. He is intentional about building a strong connection with his children, putting in effort even when faced with challenges.

He loves, protects, serves and provides for their physical and emotional needs. Expressing his love openly, he ensures that his children feel emotionally and physically safe and secure when in his presence.

Aspects of this father type are:

- Emotionally engaged with his children, openly expressing love, affection and support, he has a strong emotional bond.

- Actively listens to his children, encourages open dialogue and communicates effectively about both positive and challenging topics.
- Encourages independence, supporting decision-making, autonomy and development of essential life skills.
- Implements discipline in a fair and consistent manner, setting clear expectations and boundaries.
- Engaged in the child's educational journey, as well as recognising the importance of play.
- Celebrates achievements both big and small.
- Adaptable and flexible in response to changing needs.
- Recognises the importance of emotional expression, encouraging his children to share their feelings openly.

THE IMPACT OF THE ACTIVE FATHER

Impacts of the active father are:

Relationship Patterns

Having an actively involved father tends to foster a secure attachment, contributing to healthier relationships in adulthood. You find it easier to trust others and form deep emotional connections. Overall, you are likely to demonstrate positive relationship skills and be more adept at communication, conflict resolution and emotional expression.

The Formation of Identity

Identity formation is significantly influenced by an active father, contributing to a child's sense of self-worth and identity. As adults, you are likely to have a clearer understanding of your values, strengths and purpose. This clarity often correlates with academic excellence, increasing opportunities for success in adulthood. Additionally, you are more prone to developing strong social skills, translating into positive relationships and effective communication.

As we conclude this chapter, take a moment to contemplate how your father impacted you.

- What have you learned?
- How are you going to implement this?

Chapter 17
Healing Your Father Wounds

Acknowledge and Validate Your Feelings

Recognise and accept your feelings without judgement. It's okay to feel angry, confused, sad or any other emotions in response to your father's anger or absence. Validating your feelings is a vital step in your healing journey. Allow yourself to experience and process these emotions without judgement.

Be kind to yourself and recognise the impact of having an angry or absent father is not your fault. You deserve compassion and understanding. Treat yourself with the same kindness that you would extend to a friend facing similar challenges.

Forgiveness

Whilst forgiveness doesn't imply condoning harmful behaviour, it empowers you to release resentment for your own well-being. Endeavour to understand the circumstances surrounding your father's absence or anger, acknowledging that his choices have been influenced by various factors. Recognising that these choices do not reflect you as an individual.

Jessica, for example, came to realise that her own father's upbringing had led to his emotional absence and this understanding helped her to let go of her anger and sadness.

Build a Support System

Establish a robust support system by surrounding yourself with understanding individuals, including friends and family. Cultivating a strong support network offers comfort and encouragement, providing you with the opportunity to share your experiences and seek support when needed.

Reflection

Reflection is a potent tool for personal growth and healing. Take time to delve into your values, interests and goals, seeking to understand yourself independently of your father's anger or absence. This self-awareness can be empowering. Incorporate mindfulness activities, like deep breathing or meditation to manage stress and anxiety effectively. Prioritise self-care pursuits that bring you joy and relaxation.

Educate yourself about the impact of childhood experiences on mental health and well-being, gaining insight into the root causes of emotional pain. This knowledge empowers you to make informed decisions for your healing journey. Explore healthy outlets for expressing your emotions, whether through art, journalling or conversations with trusted friends. The goal is to release pent-up emotions and gain clarity on your feelings.

Healing Your Angry Father Wounds

Establish Boundaries

Establishing healthy boundaries with your father, if feasible, involves clear communication about acceptable behaviours and defining consequences for crossing those boundaries. These boundaries play a crucial role in safeguarding your emotional well-being.

journal

Consider using these journal prompts to aid you on your healing journey:

- Reflect on situations where you felt the impact of your father's anger. How did those incidents affect you emotionally?
- Reflect on ways you coped with your father's anger, both in the past and currently. Have these

coping mechanisms helped or are there healthier alternatives?

- Consider how your father's anger has influenced your relationships with others.
- Journal about the boundaries you'd like to establish to protect yourself emotionally. How can you effectively communicate these?
- Describe the characteristics and dynamics that would contribute to a positive connection.
- What does forgiveness mean to you, and do you feel ready to consider it as part of your healing process?

Healing Your Absent Father Wounds

Define Your Own Identity

Cultivate your individual identity by concentrating on your own interests, values and aspirations, separate from your father's influence. In the event that your absent father re-enters your life, contemplate establishing clear and healthy boundaries. Communicate your needs and expectations openly, and exercise caution in determining the level of involvement you find comfortable.

journal

Consider using these journal prompts to aid you on your healing journey:

- Reflect on how your father's absence manifested and how it impacted on you.
- Reflect on how the absence of your father has influenced your sense of self.
- How do you think your life might have been different, had your father been present?
- How have the positive relationships in your life contributed to your well-being?
- Reflect on how your father's absence has influenced your relationships with others, particularly in terms of trust, intimacy and vulnerability.
- Reflect on the strengths you've developed as a result of an absent father.

Healing Your Emotionally Absent Father Wounds

Cultivate Your Own Emotional Intelligence

Enhance your own emotional intelligence by fostering awareness of your emotions and acquiring skills to manage them effectively. This process can contribute to improved emotional well-being and empower you in your interpersonal relationships.

journal

Consider using these journal prompts to aid you on your healing journey:

- Reflect on specific incidences from your childhood that illustrate your father's emotional absence. How did these experiences shape your understanding of emotional connection?
- Reflect on how your father's emotional absence has influenced your relationship with others. Consider any challenges or strengths that have emerged in your connections with friends, family and romantic partners.
- Reflect on your emotional needs. What emotional support do you seek in relationships and how can you communicate this?
- How has your father's emotional absence impacted on your sense of self-worth? Explore any negative perceptions and challenge them with positive affirmations.

Healing Your Non-Residential Father Wounds

Given that your non-residential father will likely align with one of the previously discussed father archetypes, I haven't included specific healing tips for this category.

However, recognising the archetype your father aligns with is crucial for tailoring your healing approach. Whether dealing with an absent, active, angry or disengaged father, acknowledging the specific challenges is a key starting point.

journal

Journal prompts that might help you to heal your non-residential father wounds are:

- Reflect on your relationship with your father. What were the positive aspects? What were the challenges?
- How do you feel about the time spent together? And how do you feel about the time spent apart?
- Reflect on how your father's non-residential presence has influenced your sense of identity.
- In what ways do you feel connected or disconnected from your father?

- Reflect on your emotional needs and desires in the relationship. How can you work towards fulfilling them?

Archetypes

Once more, it is essential to recognise that these five father types are archetypes and that most fathers will embody aspects of different types. Various factors from other family members or the overall environment in which you were raised should be considered.

Additionally, I haven't provided specific healing information for the active father because this aspect of your father will not have been a significant source of pain. I encourage you to explore the prompts provided for the other four types and see if any resonate with you for meaningful reflection.

Whilst I acknowledge that aspects of both these mother and father archetypes are stereotypical, it's crucial to recognise the uniqueness of each parent and individual. The descriptions provided serve as a starting point for further exploration. Understand that everyone's experiences and qualities are diverse and multifaceted.

As we come to the end of this chapter, take time to reflect on your own experience of being Fathered and how it impacts on you in the here and now.

- What have you learned?
- How will you implement it?

Chapter 18

Siblings

According to a survey I completed, almost 80% of us grow up with at least one sibling. Despite occasional conflicts, siblings generally play positive roles in each other's lives. Although there is no concrete evidence supporting the impact of sibling order, it is undeniable that our interactions with siblings and other family members profoundly influence us.

Siblings take various forms, including traditional siblings, half-siblings, step-siblings, adopted or foster siblings, as well as other individuals whom we perceive as siblings. Personally, due to a significant age gap between my brother, sister and me, I have developed close relationships with my nieces, who in many ways have been like siblings to me.

Various factors can influence the dynamics of sibling relationships, giving rise to both positive and challenging dynamics. Key contributors are:

- **Birth Order:** The hierarchical arrangement of siblings within the family structure can shape your roles and interactions.
- **Age Gap:** The disparity in age between siblings can affect their relationship dynamics. Those with a closer age gap can share more common interests, while larger age gaps will result in distinct life stages and diverse interests.
- **Parenting Styles:** The approaches adopted by caregivers in raising siblings can have a profound impact on their relationships. Inconsistency or favouritism gives rise to competition or rivalry between siblings.
- **Family Environment:** The atmosphere within the family, encompassing warmth, communication and support, plays a crucial role in shaping sibling relationships. A positive family environment generally fosters healthier and more meaningful connections among siblings.
- **Parental Modelling:** Our understanding of relationships often stems from observing our parents. Positive role modelling in communication, conflict resolution and emotional expression can significantly contribute to fostering healthier sibling relationships.
- **Shared Experiences:** The bonds among siblings can be strengthened through shared experiences, such as family holidays, traditions or significant life events. Conversely, negative

experiences such as family conflicts, create strains in sibling relationships.

- **Individual Personalities:** The distinct personalities and temperaments of each sibling play a significant role in shaping interactions. Differences in interests, communication styles, and emotional expressions can either complement each other or present challenges in cultivating strong relationships.
- **Communication Styles:** Siblings often have diverse communication styles that impact how they express themselves and comprehend each other. The ability to understand and adapt to these differences is crucial for resolving conflicts and building robust connections.
- **Conflict Resolution:** Navigating conflicts and resolving disagreements is pivotal for the quality of sibling relationships. Developing effective conflict resolution skills contributes to healthier interactions and fosters a more positive dynamic among siblings.
- **Parental Involvement:** The extent of parental attention and involvement each sibling receives significantly influences their relationship. Feelings of favouritism or neglect can breed resentment or rivalry among siblings. Additionally, parental expectations for each sibling, whether in academics, career choices or personal decisions, have a profound effect on their relationships. The pressure to meet certain

expectations introduces tension into the dynamic.

- **Life Changes:** Major life changes, such as relocation, divorce or the arrival of a new sibling, can impact sibling relationships. Adaptations to these changes can either strengthen or strain the bond between siblings.
- **Cultural and Societal Influences:** Cultural and societal expectations play a role in shaping sibling relationships, particularly in terms of gender roles, responsibilities and adherence to family traditions. These external influences contribute to the overall dynamics within the sibling unit.
- **Jealousy and Competition:** Jealousy and competition often emerge among siblings, especially where there is a perception of unequal treatment or competition for parental attention and resources.

Sibling Types in Childhood

In the realm of childhood relationships, various sibling types contribute to family dynamics. These diverse roles collectively shape the mosaic of childhood, influencing both families and individuals. Sibling types that I've identified are:

The Surrogate Caregiver

In households where consistent parental presence is lacking, an elder sibling often steps into the role of caregiver, assuming responsibility for the welfare and necessities of younger siblings. This familial dynamic has the potential to foster maturity and instil a profound sense of responsibility in the caregiving sibling. Due to the lack of emotional maturity of this caregiver, younger siblings' emotional needs are unmet, leading to the development of an insecure attachment type.

Impact in Adulthood - As you transition into adulthood, you exhibit exceptional leadership qualities, showcasing adept conflict resolution and effective communication skills honed through your caregiving experiences. Nevertheless, you encounter difficulties in establishing boundaries and prioritising your personal needs above those of others.

The Non-Conformist

Within the familial framework, certain siblings assume the role of rebels, defying established norms of authority within the family structure. This choice serves as a means to assert their independence or garner attention, particularly in contrast to less rebellious siblings.

Impact in Adulthood - As you mature into adulthood, you are likely to cultivate a robust sense of independence and a predisposition to resist conformity. This inclination manifests in a penchant for challenging norms, thinking innovatively and rebuffing authority. While these traits pose challenges, such as navigating societal expectations and adhering to established structures, they can be wellsprings of creativity and resilience. The rebellious spirit often contributes to the development of unique perspectives, motivating individuals to carve out distinct paths and embrace autonomy.

The Family Entertainer

Within the sibling dynamic, certain individuals assume the role of the family entertainer, wielding humour as a tool to dissipate tension and command attention. Adopting a playful and outgoing demeanour, they actively engage with other family members through their light-hearted approach. Other siblings can end up feeling overshadowed.

Impact in Adulthood – As you transition into adulthood, your predisposition towards light-heartedness and sociability persists. You often carry a positive outlook on life, demonstrating the capacity to create enjoyable environments for those around you. This knack for infusing joy and humour into various situations becomes a defining feature of your adult persona, fostering a buoyant atmosphere wherever you go.

The Responsible Achiever

There may emerge an individual who consistently pursues approval and success, adopting the role of the responsible achiever. Driven to excel in academics, sports or other endeavours, this sibling is marked by their unwavering commitment to achievement.

Impact in Adulthood - As you mature into adulthood, you evolve into a conscientious and goal-oriented individual. Your journey is characterised by the manifestation of leadership qualities, adept organisational skills and a steadfast commitment to personal and professional success. As a responsible achiever, you continue to be a driving force in your endeavours, navigating challenges with determination and leaving a lasting impact in various spheres of life.

The Harmonious Mediator

Within the sibling dynamic, there can be an individual who frequently intervenes to resolve conflicts and mediate disputes, adopting the role of the peacemaker. This sibling places high value on maintaining harmony within the family, actively seeking to preserve a balanced and peaceful environment.

Impact in Adulthood - As you transition into adulthood, you will cultivate proficiency in problem-solving and mediation. With your ability to foster harmony continuing to play a pivotal role in your life, this will contribute to the development of positive relationships and position you as an adept advisor. The mediator's legacy is one of cultivating understanding, resolving differences and promoting a cooperative and supportive atmosphere.

The Guardian

Within families where one sibling requires additional support, other siblings often assume a protective and supportive role, fostering the development of empathy, patience and a sense of responsibility.

Impact in Adulthood – As you progress into adulthood, you will carry with you a robust sense of responsibility and a nurturing nature. Prioritising the well-being and safety of others becomes a defining characteristic and you will evolve into a trusted confidante with empathic qualities. Actively working to create a secure and nurturing environment, you will contribute to the establishment of a supportive and caring atmosphere, where those around you feel safeguarded and understood.

Sibling Order

The order of siblings within a family can significantly influence individual development contributing to a unique blend of personality traits and coping mechanisms, shaping each sibling's perspective and approach to life.

Oldest Child

The eldest sibling often assumes leadership roles within the family, shouldering a significant sense of responsibility and serving as an example for younger siblings.

Impact in Adulthood - In adulthood, the impact of being the oldest sibling manifests in the development of robust leadership qualities and an ingrained sense of responsibility. Your upbringing positions you naturally to take charge, offering guidance to others. This life experience equips you with effective communication skills and adept conflict resolution abilities, making you valuable contributors to collaborative efforts and fostering positive relationships in various spheres of life.

Middle Child

The middle child often finds themselves navigating between the responsibilities of the elder sibling and the attention showered on the youngest, leading them to develop a peacemaker role or a diplomatic attitude within the family structure.

Impact in Adulthood - As middle children transition into adulthood, your unique position influences you by fostering adaptability and honing peace-making skills. The experience of mediating between siblings instils a knack for diplomacy, as you seek harmony and balance in your interactions. You will become adept at navigating diverse social situations with ease, displaying flexibility and approachability that contribute to your ability to build positive connections and maintain a harmonious environment in various aspects of life.

Youngest Child

The youngest sibling often relishes the advantages of being the family's baby, leading to a more free-spirited, charming and less disciplined nature.

Impact in Adulthood - As you grow into adulthood, your birth order continues to shape you, imbuing you with charm, adaptability and a penchant for seeking attention. This upbringing fosters resourcefulness, enabling you to navigate social situations with ease. Typically, you will exhibit a positive outlook on life, coupled with a playful and carefree demeanour. These qualities contribute to your ability to approach challenges with optimism and maintain a light-hearted perspective in various aspects of your adult life.

Only Children

Only children deviate from typical sibling dynamics, forming stronger bonds with their parents. This unique upbringing often fosters independence, maturity and comfort with adult company, as they don't share their immediate environment with siblings. However, challenges in sharing and collaborating might emerge as they navigate social interactions.

Impact in Adulthood - As you transition into adulthood, the impact of your singular upbringing becomes evident. You harbour a robust sense of independence, finding solace and comfort in solitude. Self-reliance becomes a defining trait and you will value your autonomy highly. The experience of enjoying undivided attention from your parents will contribute to the development of a strong sense of self and comfort with solitude, shaping you into an individual who navigates the world with confidence and a sense of inner strength.

Twins and Other Multiples

Multiples merit special consideration and this is, a topic close to my heart as a mother of five-year-old twins and also through my experiences of working with clients who are twins, triplets or parents of multiples. The connection between multiples often involves a profound closeness, offering companionship and emotional support that significantly shapes development. The constant interaction inherent in multiples relationships contributes to the cultivation of robust social skills, although it is not without its challenges.

Multiple relationships bring their own challenges, including the need to assert their uniqueness and forge individual identities, struggles with defining boundaries, dependence issues and the inevitable comparisons made by yourself and others all alongside the typical sibling rivalry.

Impact in Adulthood - As twins or multiples transition into adulthood, the impact of your unique bond will continue to resonate, this connection often equips you with a remarkable ability to forge deep connections with others, fostering adaptability and cooperation in various social and professional contexts. This upbringing instils a heightened awareness of the importance of communication, empathy and the significance of shared experiences, shaping you into individuals who bring a rich and nuanced perspective to your interactions with the world.

Sibling types in adulthood

Sibling dynamics in adulthood can be categorised into five distinct types:

- **Intimate Siblings** - Exceptionally devoted, prioritising the sibling relationships above all others, fostering a deep and unwavering connection.
- **Congenial Siblings** - Whilst maintaining a close and caring friendship, congenial siblings place a higher value on relationships such as marriage and parent/child bonds, balancing family connections.
- **Loyal Siblings** - Grounded in a shared family history, loyal siblings consistently maintain regular contact, actively participate in family gatherings, and stand steadfastly by each other's side during times of crisis.

- **Apathetic** – This category encompasses siblings who don't feel a strong sense of connection and engage in infrequent or no contact, reflecting a more distant relationship.
- **Hostile** – Rooted in resentment and anger, hostile sibling relationships are characterised by tension and conflict, making interactions challenging and strained.

As we conclude this chapter, take a moment to contemplate how your siblings (or lack of siblings) have impacted you

- What have you learned?
- How are you going to implement this?

Chapter 19

Healing Your Sibling Wounds

Healing sibling wounds involves acknowledging past hurts, fostering open communication and cultivating empathy. Reflecting on shared experiences and addressing unresolved conflicts can pave the way for understanding and forgiveness. Establishing boundaries and setting realistic expectations for each other's growth promotes a healthier dynamic. Investing time in rebuilding trust and creating positive memories can contribute to the gradual healing of sibling wounds. Ultimately, recognising the importance of family bonds and choosing compassion over resentment allows for a renewed connection and a path towards reconciliation.

Self-Reflection

Self-reflection is a crucial step in navigating sibling relationships. Dedicate time to introspection, delving into your feelings and experiences with your siblings. Identify specific wounds, emotions and triggers, and recognise any reoccurring patterns or issues that have shaped your dynamic.

Communication and Expression

Communication is key to resolving misunderstandings and fostering healthier connections. Initiate open conversations with your siblings, sharing your feelings and experiences whilst remaining receptive to their perspectives. This two-way exchange lays the foundation for understanding and healing.

Allow yourself the freedom to express your emotions through various outlets, whether it's verbalising them in conversations, jotting them down in writing or channelling them through creative endeavours. Articulating your feelings can be a cathartic process, offering clarity on the origins of your wounds and paving the way for emotional healing and growth.

Establishing Boundaries

To nurture healthier sibling relationships, clearly articulate and communicate well-defined boundaries. Establishing these boundaries serves as a proactive measure to prevent reoccurring conflicts and sets the stage for respectful interactions. This clarity provides a framework within which both parties can navigate the relationships with mutual understanding and consideration.

Practicing Empathy and Forgiveness

Engage in an empathic journey by seeking to understand your sibling's perspective, recognising that everyone carries their own set of experiences and emotions. Cultivating empathy paves the way for a more compassionate approach to resolving conflicts. Equally important is the practice of forgiveness, not necessarily for the benefit of your sibling, but for yourself, to let go of past grievances and to liberate yourself from the burden of resentment, which is a vital step in your healing process.

Whilst acknowledging past wounds, shift your focus to the present and the potential of your future relationships. Identify shared goals and interests that can foster positive interactions and strengthen your bond. Healing is a gradual process, and relationships require time to transform. Exercise patience as you navigate through this journey of healing and understand that any positive changes won't happen overnight.

journal

- What specific emotions arise when you think about your relationship with your siblings? Identify and acknowledge these feelings.
- Describe the specific wounds or conflicts you believe exist in your relationship with your siblings.
- Explore any recurring patterns or behaviours that contribute to sibling wounds? Reflect if these patterns are rooted in specific situations or if they have become habitual?
- What positive qualities and interactions would characterise your ideal sibling relationship?
- Identify ways in which you have personally grown or changed since the wounds occurred. Has your perspective evolved? What strengths have you developed?
- How has being an only child empowered you?
- How has being an only child influenced your approach to relationships?
- How do your unique qualities and interests contribute to your distinct persona?
- Reflect on any comparisons made between you and your siblings. Consider how they have impacted your self-esteem and self-perception.

Key Considerations

It is crucial to recognise that again, the roles described in this chapter serve as archetypes and initial points for deeper exploration. You may discover aspects of yourself or your siblings that align with different types, providing a nuanced understanding of your familial dynamics. Personally, despite being the youngest child and recognising traits from that type, I can identify many of my traits in the characteristics associated with only children, due to the substantial age gap between my siblings and me.

Moreover, when delving into the process of healing family wounds, it is essential to acknowledge that this doesn't mandate fostering relationships with all family members. If a sibling or a parent poses a sense of threat or emotional distress, coercing a connection is not a healthy approach. Prioritise your own well-being and recognise that healing can manifest through setting boundaries and making choices that prioritise your safety and emotional health.

As we come to the end of this chapter, take time to reflect on your own experiences with your siblings and how it impacts on you in the here and now.

- What have you learned?
- How will you implement it?

Chapter 20

Family Structures

Families come in many shapes and sizes, each characterised by unique dynamics, structures and influences that mould us in distinct ways. The influence of families extends far beyond the confines of the immediate household, with cultural and ethnic backgrounds imprinting family values, traditions and expectations that significantly shape our perceptions of ourselves and others.

Other crucial factors come into play, such as socio-economic status, which can impact access to resources, education and opportunities. The intricate interplay between family structures and individual development emphasises the necessity of acknowledging and respecting the diversity inherent in families in our interconnected society.

Now, let's explore the various types of families:

Nuclear Family

Nuclear families consist of two parents and their children residing in a single household, forming a fundamental unit for emotional support and collaborative responsibilities. This family structure often offers a stable and predictable environment, offering routines that contribute to a sense of consistency. The smaller family size facilitates close relationships and shared activities. However, when contrasted with extended families, nuclear families tend to provide a more confined support system. The parents shoulder the responsibilities for finances, childcare and household management, leading to potential stress and fatigue.

Impacts of growing up in a nuclear family include:

- **Stability and Security** - The stability and security inherent in a nuclear family can significantly contribute to emotional well-being and a sense of safety.
- **Interpersonal Skills** - The closely-knit nature of the family encourages regular interaction, facilitating the development of effective communication skills and strong interpersonal relationships.
- **Emotional Resilience** -Within the supportive environment of a nuclear family, there is a likelihood of developing a heightened sense of emotional stability, contributing to emotional resilience.

- **Dependency on the Family Structure** – Growing up in a nuclear family leads to challenges in adapting to changes, as there can be a heightened dependency on the established family structure.
- **Pressure to Conform** – There might be societal or family expectations associated with the nuclear family model which leads to pressure to conform to traditional family roles.

Extended Family

Extended families encompass relatives beyond the nuclear unit, including grandparents, aunts, uncles and cousins. This extended network offers invaluable support and influence in the upbringing of children, providing both emotional and practical assistance. However, the diverse presence of multiple generations and personalities within extended families can lead to conflicts and tensions.

Impacts of growing up in an extended family include:

- **Strong Intergenerational Bonds** – You cultivate robust intergenerational bonds within the extended family, fostering close relationships that provide a profound sense of belonging and support. The extended family structure establishes a broader emotional support system, enhancing the overall sense of community.
- **Cultural and Family Values** – Extended families play a pivotal role in passing down cultural

traditions, values and family histories, contributing significantly to the development of a strong sense of identity and cultural connection.

- **Tensions** - The coexistence of multiple generations and diverse personalities within extended families can occasionally give rise to tensions and conflicts.
- **Role Ambiguity** - Roles and expectations are less clearly defined in extended families, presenting challenges in decision making processes and establishing clear boundaries.

Single-Parent Family

In single parent families, one parent assumes the role of the sole caregiver and provider for the children. This situation can arise through divorce, death, separation or a deliberate choice to raise children independently. These family units often cultivate strong and close bonds, as the smaller size fosters a deep sense of mutual understanding. However, the single parent also experiences emotional and financial strains, which can subsequently impact the child.

Impacts of growing up in a single-parent family include:

- **Close Parental Bonds** - Close and strong bonds are forged between children and their single parent. This connection contributes to a deep sense of trust and emotional security and lays the foundation for supportive relationships in adulthood. Additionally, the adaptability learned from a single-parent upbringing will lead to close bonds with your own children.

- **Resilience and Independence** - You will often develop resilience and independence through navigating challenges, taking on responsibilities and becoming self-sufficient.
- **Strong Work Ethic** - Single-parent families frequently emphasise the value of hard work and perseverance. If you were raised in such an environment, you will develop a strong work ethic, determination and the drive to overcome obstacles.
- **Limited Support System and Time Constraints** - Single parents, often managing multiple roles, contend with a potentially smaller support system, resulting in time constraints and feelings of isolation.
- **Well-being** - Whilst some children raised in single parent families won't experience challenges related to the absence of a second parental figure, it can impact emotional well-being.

Blended Family

A blended family arises from the new relationships formed by one or both parents, uniting children from previous partnerships. This family structure not only provides an expanded support system but brings diverse perspectives and experiences to the forefront.

However, members of blended families encounter challenges in adapting to new structures, navigating complex dynamics and fostering harmonious relationships.

Impacts of growing up in a blended family include:

- **Diversity** – Blended families are made up of members from different family backgrounds, which inherently brings diverse perspectives and experiences. Exposure to varied viewpoints fosters understanding and encourages a more open-minded approach. Additionally, these families offer an expanded support system, providing both emotional and practical support.
- **Opportunity for Growth** – individuals from blended families often encounter opportunities for growth and development. Navigating complex relationships, adapting to new family dynamics and honing effective communication skills contributes significantly to personal growth.
- **Complex Relationships** – Relationships within blended families can be intricate, requiring time and effort to establish trust and meaningful connections. Stress arises around interactions between ex-partners and co-parenting arrangements, adding layers of complexity.
- **Role Ambiguity and Loyalties** – Contending with role ambiguity and loyalty conflicts can be an issue. The undefined family roles and expectations necessitate open communication and sensitivity in navigating conflicts. The

absence of these qualities can lead to difficulties persisting into adulthood.

Queer Families

These families, like my own, have parents of the same gender or from the LGBTQIA+ community. This happens through various means, such as surrogacy, adoption or in our case, assisted pregnancy methods such as IVF. Queer families challenge conventional gender norms, advocating for a more inclusive understanding of family dynamics and parental roles. Despite positive strides, queer families encounter discrimination and external pressures through unwarranted questions and comments.

Impacts of growing up in a queer family include:

- **Open-Mindedness and Acceptance** - Children raised in queer families often cultivate a greater sense of open-mindedness and acceptance of diversity. Growing up in an environment that challenges traditional gender roles can foster inclusivity, shaping individuals who embrace a more expansive understanding of human differences.
- **Resilience** - Queer families encounter societal challenges and as a result, you will have developed resilience. Navigating and managing social attitudes becomes second nature, equipping you with the ability to face adversity with strength and adaptability.

- **Social Stigma** - Discrimination and social stigma can impact the well-being of queer families. In certain parts of the world, the availability of support networks is severely limited, underscoring the challenges these families face in finding understanding and acceptance within their communities.

Adoptive or Foster Family

Families inclusive of adopted or fostered children emerge when individuals or couples assume the vital responsibility of raising children not biologically related to them. Beyond contributing a stable and supportive environment, this familial structure enables children to join a family in ways that have not been achievable through biological means. Challenges, arise in terms of attachment, influenced by the child's background, as well as concerns related to identity and belonging.

Impacts of growing up in adoptive or foster family include:

- **Opportunity For a Fresh Start** - For children who have encountered challenges or adversity early in life, becoming part of a new family offers a chance for security and unconditional love. This opportunity contributes significantly to emotional healing, providing a foundation for a fresh start.
- **Resilience** - Those of you raised in adoptive or foster families often develop resilience as you

navigate the complexities of your unique family history, fostering strength and adaptability in the face of challenges.

- **Identity or Belonging Issues** - Some of you who were raised in foster or adoptive families grapple with questions of identity or belonging, experiencing a sense of disconnect from your roots. You feel a sense of not being good enough or unwanted.
- **Attachment and Trust** - Those of you who experienced multiple placements or early disruptions encounter difficulties in forming secure attachments and trusting others, impacting your adult relationships. The presence of potentially unaddressed grief and loss can further influence emotional well-being in adulthood.

Grandparent Headed Family

In certain instances, grandparents assume the primary caregiving role for their grandchildren, often arising from the parent's inability to provide care. This familial structure, whilst offering stability and robust emotional support for the grandchildren, can pose physical and emotional strains on the grandparents. Navigating a dual role can be challenging, exacerbated by potential generational gaps.

Impacts of growing up in a grandparent-headed family include:

- **Stability and Continuity -** This contributes to a stable and supportive environment, fostering strong intergenerational bonds that provide emotional support and strengthen family unity.
- **Social Isolation -** Grandparents raising grandchildren encounter social isolation, lacking the same peer group as parents with children of similar ages. This can impact their social life and support networks, potentially leading to alienation for the child. Bridging generational gaps in these situations necessitates patience and concerted effort.

Communal Family

In communal living arrangements, individuals opt to cohabit, sharing responsibilities, resources and child-rearing duties. This family structure places a significant emphasis on cooperation and trust, fostering an environment where members provide companionship, understanding and encouragement. However, challenges arise concerning a lack of privacy, as well as potential conflicts and disagreements.

Impacts of growing up in a communal family include:

- **Shared Responsibilities -** Task-sharing within a communal setting not only promotes cooperation but cultivates valuable skills in teamwork and equitability.
- **Emotional Support** - In communal living, community members play a crucial role in

providing companionship, understanding and encouragement during both joyous and challenging times. This support contributes to a solid emotional foundation.

- **Dependency Issues** – While communal living offers a supportive environment, there is a potential risk of fostering dependency. This can pose challenges, especially if it inhibits individual autonomy. Moreover, if you were not encouraged to make independent decisions during childhood, you encounter difficulties in exercising this ability during childhood.

Military Family

Military families encounter distinctive challenges characterised by frequent relocations, deployments and the demands of service. Navigating the complexities of military life, these families often cultivate strong bonds and resilience. A robust sense of community and support emerges, complemented by travel that fosters personal growth, a broader world view and adaptability. However, challenges persist, including disruptions to stability, periods of separation and emotional stress.

Impacts of growing up in a military family include:

- **Sense of Community** – Military families frequently foster a robust sense of community where shared experiences and challenges contribute to the development of strong, resilient bonds. These connections play a significant role in fostering a profound sense of belonging.

- **Resilience Development** - Owing to the frequent moves and challenges inherent in military life, individuals from military families often develop resilience, becoming adept at adjusting to new environments and navigating the complexities of their dynamic lifestyle.
- **Instability Challenges** - The frequent relocations, separations and uncertainty experienced by military families can result in emotional stress, practical burdens and a pervasive sense of instability.

As we conclude this chapter, take a moment to contemplate how your family structure has impacted you.

- What have you learned?
- How are you going to implement this?

Chapter 21

Healing Your Family Wounds

In addition to previously discussed healing methodologies, there exists a broad spectrum of approaches relevant to the intricate process of healing from family dynamics. Engaging in reflective practices, fostering forgiveness and prioritising self-care remain crucial components of this journey.

However, an expanded perspective emphasises the importance of extending your support network beyond the familial realm. Establishing connections outside of your immediate family can introduce fresh perspectives, offer valuable advice and provide a well-rounded network of emotional support.

Boundaries

Establishing boundaries with your family is a vital aspect of maintaining healthy relationships and ensuring your well-being. Setting clear and firm boundaries involves communicating your needs, limits and expectations in a respectful manner. It is important to identify which behaviours or interactions are acceptable to you and which cross personal boundaries. This includes specifying the level of involvement you are comfortable with, expressing topics that are off limits or expressing the need for personal space and time. Communicate your boundaries calmly and assertively, emphasising that they are crucial for maintaining a positive and respectful connection. Be consistent in enforcing these boundaries, as this helps establish a sense of predictability and mutual respect.

Setting boundaries is not about creating distance but rather about fostering healthy communication and ensuring that relationships remain supportive and nurturing. It is a proactive step towards creating an environment where everyone's needs and feelings are acknowledged and respected.

Cultivating Empathy Within Family Dynamics

An essential facet of the healing process involves building empathy within the familial sphere. Beyond individual self-reflection, understanding the perspectives and experiences of family members is paramount. This intentional effort not only fosters a deeper comprehension of their viewpoints but serves as a foundation for compassion. By acknowledging and empathising with the unique journeys of each family member, the potential for improved relationships emerges, creating a more harmonious and interconnected familial dynamic.

A crucial aspect to bear in mind is the acknowledgement that the discussed family types serve again as archetypes, providing generalised frameworks rather than exhaustive categorisations. Within the intricate tapestry of family dynamics, it is entirely plausible to discover facets of your own familial structure that transcend conventional boundaries.

An illustration of this lies in the realisation that a nuclear family, traditionally defined, can concurrently embody the characteristics of a queer or military family. The fluidity of familial experience is such that a military family, known for its distinctive challenges, can incorporate elements of a blended family. These intersections highlight the multifaceted and diverse nature of family dynamics. It's important to note, for example, that a seemingly positive nuclear family can be made up of an angry father and a perfectionist mother. Families are extremely complex beasts. I urge you to view these archetypes merely as starting points for a more nuanced exploration of the diverse and intricate facets that constitute your unique family narratives.

journal

Journal prompts to heal your family wounds are:

- How do you currently feel about your family relationships?
- Are there specific emotions or patterns that consistently arise?
- Are there any generational patterns that you'd like to understand better?
- How can you advocate for yourself and your wellbeing within your family?
- Is there anyone in your family that you need to forgive? Including yourself?
- Reflect on your boundaries. Are there any areas where you need to set clearer boundaries? How can you communicate these boundaries assertively and compassionately?
- Are there aspects of your family history that bring a sense of pride or joy?
- How do your family typically express emotions or resolve conflicts?
- In what ways have challenges in your family shaped your character?
- Identify aspects of your family for which you are grateful?

As we conclude this chapter, take a moment to contemplate how your family structure has impacted you and how you can start to heal from it.

- What have you learned?
- How are you going to implement this?

Before You Go

It's essential for me to emphasise that if anything within the contents of this book stirs any emotions or triggers a response that you find challenging, I strongly encourage you to reach out to someone for support. Whether it's a trusted friend, a family member or a qualified therapist, engaging in open dialogue can provide a valuable outlet for processing and navigating any emotional challenges that arise during your reading journey. Your well-being is of utmost importance, and seeking assistance from those around you can contribute significantly to a positive and supportive experience.

I want to reiterate that just because our families have caused us pain, doesn't mean they had bad intentions, my mum is an amazing human and a brilliant mother, but sometimes, she got it wrong. I always try to be the best I can be as a parent, but I get it wrong and I'm sure if my daughters become parents, they too will sometimes get it wrong. The nature of us as humans is that we make mistakes, and that's okay. The purpose of this book is not to cast blame, but to break cycles and to help you to heal from your family's best intentions.

Positive Affirmations

Positive affirmations act as a tool to boost well-being. By consistently repeating positive statements, you nurture a more optimistic mindset, fostering confidence and resilience. Embracing this practice which I've touched on a number of times creates a constructive internal dialogue that influences your thoughts and behaviours, contributes to an overall positive and fulfilling life. To conclude this book, I'd like to leave you with positive affirmations which you can use yourselves to shift your own inner narrative.

My feelings and needs matter

All feelings are welcome

It's okay to make mistakes, that's how you learn

I deserve the space and freedom to do all the things I love

It's safe to be authentic

I deserve to be praised and encouraged

I deserve healthy relationships that honour my boundaries

I am enough

I deserve to take up space

I am strong, beautiful and kind

I choose to let go of what no longer serves me

I choose peace, stillness and rest

I am right where I'm supposed to be

No is a complete sentence

I am worthy of love and respect

I release any shame and doubt

I have experienced challenges, but they have made me more resilient

I am capable of making healthy choices

I am proud of myself

I am a cycle-breaker

References

Philip Larkin, *This Be The Verse*, 1971

John Bowlby, *A Secure Base*, 2005

The Attachment Project: Learn Attachment Theory from Experts - Accessed December 2023

Jeffery Young, Janet Klosko et al, *Schema Therapy: A Practitioner's guide*, 2006

The Emotion Wheel: What It Is and How to Use It (positivepsychology.com) – Accessed January 2023

Gary Chapman, The Five Love languages, 2014

BAM Printing House, Shadow work, 2022

Carl Jung and Tim Newcomb, The Analysis of Dreams, 2023

The five mother types | Psychologies – Accessed October 2023

The 5 Types of Dads - All Pro Dad – Accessed October 2023

The Sibling Relationship | Psychology Today – Accessed November 2023

Types of Sibling Relationships - HealthyChildren.org - Accessed November 2023

8 Types of Family Structures & Their Characteristics (wikihow.com) – Accessed December 2023

What are the Different Family Structures? (lifefamilyfun.com) – Accessed December 2023

About the Author

Lianne Terry is a Psychotherapist who employs Cognitive-Behavioural Therapy (CBT) and Person-Centred Therapy (PCT) to aid clients who are struggling to find happiness. As a qualified counsellor, she specialises in exploring relationships, family dynamics and the process of healing childhood wounds.

Having embarked on her own journey to happiness and self-empowerment by addressing past pain, Lianne is familiar with the challenges of coping with anxiety stemming from past wounds. She understands the experience of carrying pain without a clear understanding of its origin and the effort required to unravel and rebuild from it.

Today, Lianne considers herself content and fulfilled, living the life she once envisioned while managing her own private counselling practice. She is dedicated to assisting her clients in discovering joy, healing their emotional wounds and forging happy and successful lives. Lianne's approach is characterised by its gentleness and warmth, with a strong emphasis on the therapeutic relationship.

She extends empathy, candour and unwavering positive regard to each of her clients, providing a secure environment for personal growth. Lianne's clients frequently describe her as incredibly reflective, dynamic, approachable, constructive and uplifting; she possesses the ability to create a safe space for self-reflection while offering support for personal growth.

Collaborating with Lianne will afford you the opportunity to establish a deeper connection with yourself, enhance self-awareness, and find a place where your voice is heard, and your presence acknowledged.

Working With Me

You can find out more about Lianne Terry and the services she provides, including 1-2-1 counselling, her membership and speaking or training on her website:

www.lianneterrycounselling.co.uk

Or through contacting her via email at:

lianne.terry@outlook.com

You can also follow her on social media at:

https://www.facebook.com/lianne.flood

https://www.instagram.com/the_happiness_collective_/

Or join her community at:

https://www.facebook.com/groups/1054052145228126/

Printed in Great Britain
by Amazon

47631318R00165